‖‖ ‖ ‖‖‖‖‖‖‖ ‖ ‖ ‖‖‖‖‖‖‖‖‖‖‖‖‖‖‖ ‖‖

W9-BNL-025

DR. HENRY CLOUD

the Secret Things of God

Unlocking the Treasures Reserved for You

HOWARD BOOKS
A DIVISION OF SIMON & SCHUSTER
New York   London   Toronto   Sydney

Our purpose at Howard Books is to:
- *Increase faith* in the hearts of growing Christians
- *Inspire holiness* in the lives of believers
- *Instill hope* in the hearts of struggling people everywhere

Because he's coming again!

Published by Howard Books, a division of Simon & Schuster, Inc.
1230 Avenue of the Americas, New York, NY 10020

www.howardpublishing.com

The Secret Things of God © 2007 Dr. Henry Cloud

In association with the agency of Dupree/Miller & Associates, Inc.

The Library of Congress Cataloging-in-Publication Data is available.

ISBN 13: 978-1-4165-6360-0
ISBN 10:   1-4165-6360-1
10 9 8 7 6 5 4 3 2 1

Names and identifying circumstances and descriptions have been changed to protect the anonymity of individuals described in story illustrations herein.

Manufactured in the United States of America

For information regarding special discounts for bulk purchases, please contact: Simon & Schuster Special Sales at 1-800-456-6798 or business@simonandschuster.com.

Edited by Philis Boultinghouse
Cover design by LUCAS Art & Design and Stephanie D. Walker

Interior design by John Mark Luke Designs

Contents

{ CONTENTS }

$\mathscr{W}$ELCOME

You may have picked up this book because you've read or heard of *The Secret* by Rhonda Byrne. In that book, Byrne explores our relationship to the universe and how understanding what lies beyond the veil drastically affects our lives, relationships, and goals. The fact that millions have responded to *The Secret* shows the deep hunger we all have for two things: one, we all want to understand the nature of the universe and those things beyond what we can see; and, two, we all have a hunger for principles and practices that make life work.

While so many have found *The Secret*'s message to be intriguing and inspiring, it has raised several questions from those of the Judeo-Christian faith: (1) Are the forces that control the universe and our lives *impersonal and detached*, as *The Secret* explains; or is the force behind it all of a more personal nature? (2) Is there just *one secret*; i.e., your thoughts create your life, good or bad? Or, just like in the physical universe, does the spiritual universe have a *set of laws* that make life work? (3) Is making your life work all up to you; or is it a *collaborative effort* between you and a force greater than you, who cares about you and has a plan for you? It is these questions and more that *The Secret Things of God* will address.

This book is not a Christian argument for or against *The Secret.* In fact, it sometimes agrees with and sometimes differs with it. Over and above being a discussion on the principles of *The Secret,* this book affirms the deep spiritual hunger that the success of Byrne's book has shown all of us to have. And it offers tested spiritual truths based on the Bible that help *make life work.* For all of us long to know what more is out there, who this force is, how it works, how we can get on the right side of it, and if it has a name.

Today's spiritual environment reminds me of that of ancient Greece, where all kinds of spiritual discussions and ideas floated around. When the apostle Paul entered the scene, rather than bash those with different perspectives, he affirmed the quest itself. He basically said to them, "I see that you are a spiritual people, building an altar to an Unknown God. This Unknown God is who I've come to tell you about." He told them one of the things I want to share with you: God wants a relationship with you; he wants you to seek after him and to find him. Even further, he said our very existence and purpose is wrapped up in him.[1]

This book's title comes from a letter the apostle Paul wrote. In it he said, "Regard us . . . as those entrusted with the secret things of God."[2] These secrets are, indeed, a great trust—a treasure that can literally change your life. The spiritual truths shared in these pages will connect you with the God who created the universe and will unlock the secrets to *making life work.*

THE SEARCH

THE BEGINNINGS OF MY OWN SEARCH . . .

It was the spring semester of my sophomore year in college. I was at the end of my efforts to figure it all out. I had a failed dating relationship, a failed dream, and I was failing at getting out from under the depression that haunted me every day. I was at the end of my rope.

On this particular Sunday afternoon, I was sitting in my dorm room, just thinking. I was thinking about how I had come to college with high hopes in all three of those areas of life. Just a year and a half before, I was full of dreams and optimism. As I headed off to college, I was looking forward to a satisfying relational life, after going through the usual hit-and-miss of adolescent dating. I had hoped to accomplish my dream of a successful college golf career, and I had certainly hoped that all of that would bring me happiness. But after the breakup, a hand injury affected my golf game to the extent that I was not playing well enough to continue. The loss of both made it a struggle to even get up and going each day, and I was painfully aware of the gap between where I had thought I would be and where I was. And that gap was huge.

So there I was, pondering it all. I was wondering, *How do you make it all work?* How did people find the right person to fall in love with? How did they find that special path for their real talents and gifts that would become a meaningful and successful career? Forget meaningful . . . how did they even make a living? And how did they achieve happiness? What was the trick? What was the "secret" to making it all go well?

Now at this point, I was not what you would call religious, by any stretch. I would not even call myself spiritual, which at the very least means someone who puts time, thought, and effort into developing a spiritual self in some significant way. I was just a guy trying to find my way and make it all work. So understand, I was not approaching my situation that day with any sort of spiritual hopes, plans, or thoughts that God was going to reach out of the sky and make it all better. That was not a part of my experience base, so what happened next was a total shock to me. I had no idea that everything was about to change—forever.

As I sat there on my bed, pondering all these things of life, I looked around the room, and up on my bookshelf was my Bible. I felt some sort of pull, or intrigue, or a wondering if it might have something to say to me in my dilemma. However you would describe that impulse, I had not felt it before; for I had not taken that Bible off the shelf since I had come to college. But there it was, so I walked over and picked it up.

Then it happened. I opened it up, randomly, and my eyes fell

immediately to a verse that seemed to jump off the page. Here is
what it said:

> But seek first his kingdom
> and his righteousness,
> and all these things will be given to you as well.[1]

"All these things?" What things? What was it talking about? I
looked at the verses before that one, and it was talking about all the
things of life, all the stuff we worry about, like the things that I was
concerned with that day . . . like my entire future. Then it said this:

> Therefore, do not worry about tomorrow,
> for tomorrow will worry about itself.
> Each day has enough trouble of its own.[2]

Wait, I thought. Let me read that again. What it was saying was
that if I would seek God and "his kingdom and his righteousness,"
then all of this stuff would somehow work out? Is that what I was
reading? Could that be true? At that point, I had no clue what his
kingdom or righteousness even were, but I got the gist. It was telling
me that I should not worry about all the stuff I was worrying about;
but instead, I should seek God and *he* would make it all work.

For a nonreligious fraternity type, this was beyond anything I
could actually believe would work. But I was not beyond having
a wish for it to work. I mean, who wouldn't want that? A life that

actually worked because God was working things out? It felt a little like wishful thinking to me, but my way certainly was not working. So I was confronted with a choice. Should I try the "God thing"?

I have to admit, my first thought about "seeking God" was that there was no way I was going to turn into one of those religious types. I thought they were weird and definitely *not* the kind of people I could ever see myself hanging out with. Weren't they the ones who didn't even party? I knew that would never work. But I decided that I had to put all that aside and take one step: I had to find out if God was there. Then if it turned out that he was, the next step would be to see if he would help me without making me weird. That sounded like a plan. So I decided to go for it. I would "seek God," to see if this could work.

Figuring I could not do this in a dorm room, I wandered across the SMU campus and found an empty chapel. It was cold and dark, and I went down to the altar and said a simple prayer. It was something like this: "God . . . I don't even know if you are there. But if you are, I need your help. If you help me, I will do anything you tell me to do. Just help me. Find me." At that point, I knew something had changed.

No—nothing happened. No lights, no burning bush, no feelings of peace. Just empty silence. Nothing on the outside was different, but I knew that inside something had changed. I had just taken a real step of faith . . . and I knew that if God did not show up in some real way, my life had just gotten a lot worse. I knew that if he did not answer me, I was truly alone in the universe. All my life I'd had the good ol' American security blanket of "There is a God out there who is nice and loves us." But now, I had actually stepped out and asked him to do something. It's one thing to believe in God and have the security of thinking he exists, even if you have never tested that faith or done anything about it. At least you can believe he's there and take some bit of naive comfort in that. But once you step out of the boat, I thought, you'll find out whether or not he is. And if he doesn't respond, even the little faith you have is gone. It's one thing to have a faith you don't use. It's quite another not to even have an untested faith you can fall back on if you ever decide you want to. I had jumped in.

> I KNEW THAT IF GOD DID NOT SHOW UP IN SOME REAL WAY, MY LIFE HAD JUST GOTTEN A LOT WORSE.

So far, not so good. No lights, no zapping, no nothing.

So I just left the church and went back to my room. The emptiness was huge, and I tried not to think about it. What I did not realize was that my entire life was about to change. After I got back to my dorm room, the phone rang. It was a fraternity brother whom I had not talked to in a while. What he said floored me. "Okay, you are the last person I would think of calling about this, but for some reason, you kept coming to mind. We're starting a Bible study, and I wanted to see if you would like to come."

It was not hard for me to connect the dots and realize that God had heard my prayer. "I will be there," I said. "Tell me when."

I went, and it was there I began to discover that what that verse said was true.

THE SEARCH FOR REAL ANSWERS TO REAL QUESTIONS

Fast forward about twenty-five years . . . I was sitting on an airplane just enjoying the idea of a few hours of quiet time . . . no kids, no phone, no work. Just a little space in the air to relax, ignore a cheesy movie, and read a good book. Then it happened, my worst in-flight nightmare . . . even worse than bad turbulence. The woman sitting next to me turned to strike up a conversation. On this particular day, that was the last thing I wanted. But she looked at me and asked, "So, what do you do?"

Usually, when caught in those kinds of crosshairs, I pull out my secret weapon for making unwanted airplane conversations disappear. I say, "I am an author. I write books about God." Almost without exception, that buys me an immediate three hours of silence, as people give some sort of nice nod and raise their newspapers back up to pages they have already read. It always gets me off the hook. But I must have been off my game that day, because I said, "Oh, I am a psychologist."

Wrong answer. She immediately said, "Oh, my gosh. I have to tell you about my boyfriend. I need help. I am just stuck and don't know what to do. I love him so much, but . . ." She went on to tell me about her relationship with a guy she was very much in love with but who was pretty self-centered and would get angry when he did not get his way. She described a cycle: Whenever she would say "no" to him, he would get mad, the controlling behavior would escalate, and they would have a big disconnect. She would feel alone and far away.

"So what do you do then?" I asked.

"Well, I can't stand it when we have a disagreement like that, and I feel so far away from him. I usually just give in, and that makes it okay between us; and we're fine after that. But it keeps happening a lot, and I just don't know if I can do this anymore. But I really like him."

"Makes sense that it keeps happening, though," I said. "You know, there is an old saying that goes, 'Do not rescue an angry man, or you will have to do it again tomorrow.' If you give in, the cycle will only continue—usually for years."

"Oh, my gosh!" she said. "That is an amazing saying, that thing about 'rescuing an angry man.' That is *so* true. Where did you get that?"

"It's in the Bible," I said.

"What? The Bible?"

"Yeah. Proverbs 19:19. Check it out."

"No way! I did not know stuff like that was in the Bible. I will have to check that out."

We went on to talk more about her rescuing patterns of giving in to the temper tantrums of this three-year-old in a thirty-five-year-old body, and it actually was a nice conversation and hopefully helpful to her. But it really had an impact on me. It almost became a defining moment for how I now like to spend a lot of my time and why I wanted to write this book. Why?

THAT CAME FROM THE BIBLE?

It was the look on her face when I told her that the saying came from the Bible. She just looked at me, sort of stunned, almost with a blank stare that said, "What? Something that was 'exactly right where I am at' came from the Bible?" She was surprised in a way that was very pure and yet said volumes. The things that it said to me reverberated in my soul and are three things that I am continually amazed at.

First of all, *she was stunned at the accuracy of how the Bible spoke directly to her situation.* As a psychologist, after years of practice and working with lots of people and overseeing the treatment of many more, I am blown away in situation after situation when I see the "secret things of God" validated by research and clinical practice. One example is how the whole codependency movement has helped millions of people find better lives and relationships through the application of just that one verse I mentioned to her. Marriages and relationships are healed every day when other principles from the Bible are applied correctly in those contexts. The most successful, researched, and proven treatments for depression, anxiety, and addictions are all right out of the Bible. In fact, I do not know of any successful clinical process or practice that does not agree with God's secrets. And in business, financial wizards make billions of dollars through practicing the principles of finance and investment taught right in the Scriptures.

So, almost every day I share her amazement at how God's secrets speak to life. To her it was a surprise. At this point in my life, it is a little more like, *well, there it is again.* Not to mention the validation of God's secrets that I have experienced in my own life over and over again since that first day in my dorm room when I wondered if God was really there. It is uncanny how God's secrets make life work, but it

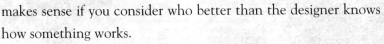

IT WAS THE LOOK ON HER FACE WHEN I TOLD HER THAT THE SAYING CAME FROM THE BIBLE.

makes sense if you consider who better than the designer knows how something works.

Secondly, I am amazed every day at *how surprised people are that those things are actually in the Bible.* I do not in any way mean this as pejorative, but so many of us are just unaware of what is actually in there. I was, if you recall my story from the beginning of this prologue. In my search to figure it all out, I just did not know that God had a promise in there about how to order life. And, I found later, I was unaware of countless other life-changing secrets that were in there as well. But I guess what surprises me still is that while so many of us know "about" the Bible, we just don't know much "of" the Bible.

And the third thing I am always moved by, are the *preconceptions that people have about the Bible*, which showed on her face as well. It said something like, *"I didn't know there was anything in there that I would even be interested in."* Though people are searching for meaning and answers, so many still see the Bible as a book of myths and fables and as antiscientific, outdated, religious, and moralistic. Then when they find out it may actually contain something helpful, it bumps up against their preconceptions.

The reason this one moves me is that so many people come by that opinion honestly. They have seen weird Christians on TV or even stranger ones in real life, and from those experiences have decided that the whole Christianity thing must be wacky. I remember thinking a long time ago that I did not have a problem with God; it was his friends I couldn't relate to. So when I talk to people about God and find out they have lost interest in him because of goofy expressions of faith by strange people, I always want to say, "Don't do that!"—don't get turned off because of one weirdo or one bad experience. That would be like going out to eat, having a bad meal, and deciding to never go to another restaurant.

ENTER *THE SECRET*...

I first heard about *The Secret* by Rhonda Byrne from a good friend of mine. He knew that I was into spiritual things, and he said the book was a huge phenomenon and that I should read it. He said that everyone from Oprah to his kids were into it. So I picked up a copy and put it in my stack of things to read the next time the person I was sitting next to on an airplane didn't have a controlling boyfriend. I remember being interested, but didn't know what was to come next.

What did come was a call from a literary agent saying that the publisher was looking for a Christian to write a similar book from a Judeo-Christian perspective, one that described the "Secret" according to the Bible, and wanted to know if I would be interested. I told them I would look into it, and when I did, I got very interested.

I got intrigued because I found that the *interest* in the book was telling an even bigger story than *The Secret* itself. *The story that grabbed me was the huge interest people have in spiritual things.* While *The Secret* is a book about getting what you want in life, it is also a book that looks beyond a logical plan to reach your goals. It searches for a spiritual and metaphysical reality that transcends the everyday lives most people lead. It says that there are spiritual realities that govern the universe and that those are as real as the physical laws that we all live by, like gravity. And people are reading it by the millions.

Certainly, part of the appeal is that people want to know how to get the things they want out of life. I can relate to that, as that day in my dorm room reveals. But I think we all want more than that too. I think the interest in the book tells us that we all have a spiritual side to us, too, and that we all are searching for something more than ourselves and long to be connected to Someone greater. We long to be connected to something beyond the material universe we see, touch, and feel. We long to know the things that are beyond our sight. We want to know the real secrets of it all. If there is more, we want to connect with it.

And that is why I am writing this book. I believe that, as *The Secret* says, there is more to life than just what we see in front of us. It is true that the visible things we see and attain do not begin in the visible world, but the *invisible* world. If you reach your goals, you do so because spiritual principles are at work. If you find a fulfilling relationship, it is not just because a friend sets you up or you find a good dating service. There are invisible laws at work. If you overcome depression or addiction, it is not just because you tried harder. It is because spiritual realities are involved. The Creator of the universe who set it all up has built into life spiritual laws that are as real as physical laws, like gravity, and *when we get on the right side of those laws, life just works better.*

In this book, I want to show some of the most powerful secrets of God that affect the kinds of things that psychologists worry about . . . and that you care about:

- how you feel

- how your relationships work

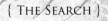

- how you reach your goals and dreams

- how to make life work

- how to find and know God

In addition, this book will also discuss how some principles in *The Secret* relate to principles in the Bible, where the Bible goes even further, and where the Bible has a different perspective from *The Secret*. I think it will be a fun exercise and interesting for you to not only discover some of the "secret things of God" that you did not know were there (without the plane ride) but to also compare how people of different faith perspectives talk about some of the same issues. It will also be interesting and helpful for those of you who have known some of these secrets all your faith-life, yet still don't know how to make them *work* in your life. We're going to talk about how to do that.

I hope that no matter where you are in your search—whether to find God for the first time or to get to know him even better—you find three things in this book. First, that God is very real and loves you very much, no matter what you might have heard. Second, that he does have some secrets for us that really, really do work. And third, if you're like me, you'll be glad to know that you don't have to be very religious to enjoy both of those realities. Just be open and real as you go through this journey. God will do the rest. Let's go.

No matter where you are in your faith journey— whether you are just testing the waters to see if there is anything out there worth believing in or you are a longtime believer desiring a richer, more fulfilling relationship with the Creator of the universe—the starting point is always the same. Seek. This is where it all begins.

Seek and you will find.

the Secret Revealed

ℐf You Seek God, He Will Show Up

*"You will seek me and find me when you seek
me with all your heart.
I will be found by you," declares the* LORD.

—JEREMIAH 29:13–14 NIV

The secret to finding God is to seek him out. It's that simple.

One of the draws of *The Secret* has been that anyone, any-where can reach out to the universe and it will respond. This has touched a spiritual chord in millions of readers. One of the main differences in the Judeo-Christian faith and others is that the One we reach out to is a personal God who knows us individu-ally and cares about us. This God makes an absolute guarantee that *anyone* who wants to find him will. There is no trick, no gimmick, no maze or standard that those who desire him must negotiate. He promises that if we want to find him, we will. How can we be so sure? *Because he is looking for us and always has been.* That is the secret to finding God in the Judeo-Christian faith. We will find him because he wants to be found—even more than that, he is trying to find us each and every day.

THEY LOOKED FOR GOD . . . AND HE SHOWED UP

It seemed like just another day on the *New Life Live!* radio show, with callers asking questions about the kinds of issues we talk about on that program. But then a young man called with a different kind of question and a different kind of pain.

With a quivering voice and holding back his tears, he began to ask questions that you could tell were coming from the very depths of his soul. Our conversation went something like this:

"I have been listening to you guys, and I just don't understand how you can talk about God like that . . ."

"What do you mean?" I asked.

"Well, you talk about him like you know he is there . . . and like you know who he is . . . I mean, there are so many religions, so many faiths, and the Bible . . . How can you know for sure he is there? How do you know which god is the real God?"

"Let me ask you something," I said. "Do you *want* to know? I mean *really* want to know?"

"Why, sure . . . very much so. I would love to know that God is there and who he is."

"I ask because a lot of people wonder about God, and they think about him a lot. They discuss and debate about him with their friends, all the while thinking they would like to know whether or not he exists, but kind of from an intellectual place. But God says that if you really want to know him and who he is and have a relationship with him, then you can. And he says that if you seek him, you will find him—if you sincerely seek him with your whole heart. So I am asking you, do you really want to know?"

"Yes . . . I do," he said.

"Okay, here is what I want you to do. Forget all of your wondering, all of your thoughts, all of your doubts. Wherever you are, right now, I just want you to ask him to please show you. Put that much belief in him. Ask him to show you who he is and what his name is. Tell him that you want to know him, and ask him to find you. If you do that, and mean it, he will hear you. You will find him."

"That's it? That's all I have to do?" he asked.

"That's all you have to do," I said. "But you have to do it from a sincere heart. And after you do, let us know what happens."

He later called us back and told us that he had come into a real relationship with God, all beginning with that phone call. As exciting as that was, something else was happening as a result of that call in an entirely different part of the country. Someone else had been listening, and that led to another encounter of an amazing kind. For shortly after that call on the radio, I got a very interesting message on my daily message list. It said:

A woman from Boston called and said that you said on the radio that you like to talk to non-Christians about God, and she would like to talk to you. She is coming to L.A. and would like to meet with you.

First of all, I wondered how the message got through to my list. Since the show is nationally syndicated, our call center receives over twenty thousand calls a month, and there is an entire staff that handles the calls that originate from the radio. I do not see them, first of all because there are just too many, and secondly, I am not the one they need to talk to. They usually need to be connected with help in their area, a resource, a workshop, or assistance from our team. So it was unusual for this to come through to my assistant as that is not the normal routing of calls. But somehow it did.

I DO NOT KNOW HOW TO EXPLAIN THIS, BUT THERE WAS SOMETHING *DIFFERENT* ABOUT THAT MESSAGE AS IT SAT ON THE PAGE.

Next, I would not normally be able to meet with someone who just wanted to discuss something I said on the radio; there are just too many questions and not enough time. But, and I do not know how to explain this, there was something *different* about that message as it sat on the page. It just seemed to stand out in some different kind of way. I was drawn to it. So I asked my assistant to call her back and tell her that I would like to meet with her.

At that point, I got a little bit of a push-back from my assistant, who knew I was already overcommitted and was looking to find some time, not lose more. So she said something like "No . . . you can't do that. Let someone else talk to her. You need to finish such and such a project, and you are running out of time," or some similar assistant scolding, which is what a good assistant does when her boss puts more into his schedule than he should. But that message was different . . . I just felt it. So I pushed back at her, "No, I really want to see what this is about. Set it up." So she did.

Helene came to my office, introduced herself, and we sat down to talk. I was instantly impressed with her spirit and her authenticity. She seemed "real."

"So, how can I help you?" I asked.

"Well, you said on the radio that you like to talk to 'non-Christian people' about God, right?"

"Yes, that's right. Does that mean you?" I asked.

"Yes, it does."

"What would you like to talk about?" I inquired.

"Do you remember a few weeks ago when you told that guy in his car that if he wanted to find out if God was there and who he was to just ask him?"

"Yes, I do, actually. I loved that call."

"Well, I did that," she said. "And now I have a problem."

"You did? What happened? Tell me."

"I had just returned from the doctor's office where I had gotten a really bad diagnosis . . . cancer. I was devastated and really, really scared. I have never felt like that before. So I did what you said. I got down on my knees and just asked. I said, 'If there is anybody out there . . . help me. Whoever you are, if there is a God, just please help me.'"

"So, what happened?" I asked.

"When I did that, and this is going to sound crazy . . . Jesus came to me," she said.

"*He did?*" I asked.

"Yes," she said. "He did."

"How?"

"Well, it is difficult to describe, but it was like he surrounded me in a warm . . . peaceful . . . loving . . . bubble. I was engulfed in it, and *he was there*. And I knew it was Jesus. There is no doubt about it. And he held me there for a little while—I am not sure how long—and he told me that it was going to be okay. Then he just held me there for a little while longer. It was the most peaceful, loving feeling and presence I have ever felt. I cannot even describe it. And then, after a little while, he left. That was it."

I was stunned, moved, riveted, and also overwhelmed at the genuineness with which she told her story. There was no drama, just a sincere account of an amazing encounter. I knew it was real.

She was not psychotic or delusional or manic. I am a psychologist, and I knew I was talking to a very sane CPA—logical and fully there. All I could muster was a "Wow." But her story did leave me with a big question.

"That is amazing . . . so what's your problem?" I really thought that some-one who had been visited by Jesus and told that all was okay would be the last person to have a problem. I wish

"I ASKED FOR GOD . . . AND *JESUS* SHOWED UP."

he would come tell me that at times! What could her problem be?

"Well, my problem is that I asked for God to help me."

"Yes," I said, still not getting what the problem was.

"I asked for God . . . and *Jesus* showed up."

"Yeah . . . that would be who would show up if you asked for God," I said.

"But I'm Jewish."

Now I got it. Now I understood why she had a "problem."

"Well, if you think about it, the Bible says that there were a lot of Jews who were surprised that Jesus was the one who showed up when they were looking for God!" We had a good laugh for a moment, but then we had one of the most memorable spiritual conversations I have ever had.

For a long time we sat together, and I walked her through all of the Hebrew scriptures that she had learned years ago. We talked about the Passover, the Lamb, the sacrifices, and how the Jews knew the coming Messiah would be the Passover Lamb and that he provided forgiveness for all of our mistakes, large and small. And that Lamb would be called Immanuel, which means "God with us." And Jesus was the one who fulfilled all those prophecies and also proved he was God through his miracles and through coming back to life after he had been crucified. She came to see that what, or whom, she had experienced *was exactly what the Bible said she should have experienced*, especially as a Jew. It all made sense to her, that Jesus was the God she had reached out to.

That was a few years ago, and we have kept in touch since then. Recently she called and said she was at another scary time in her life and felt far away from God. She even laughed at herself in light of her previous experience. We talked about how she felt and how the psalmists felt the same way at times—that God sometimes seemed far away and silent. I told her I had been through times like that as well and that the Bible even says there will be times when we look for God but it seems he is not there. So I told her how important it is to get some time alone with God and just talk. To sit with him day after day and read through some psalms and other scriptures. To talk to him and pour out her heart. And I told her that God would talk to her if she did that. I didn't know how he would, but I knew he would. He promises us that. A week later, I got an e-mail that said this:

I am hearing him talk to me (although, unfortunately, not as obviously as the last time). Thank you for pointing that out; that was what I was missing.

I love her sincerity in seeking God. It touches me, and it also touches me to know that we have a God whose biggest "secret" is not a secret at all: "If you seek me, you will find me." This is the *first secret* and one that we can always depend on. Not only can I depend on that secret for myself, but I can feel confident in telling others that if they seek him, he will show up for them too.

WHAT'S YOUR "GOD STORY"?

One of my favorite things is asking people to tell me their "God story." Everyone's God story is different, and their stories show how he meets us where we are, in just the way we need.

My God story began when I asked him to help me and he sent a fraternity brother who called me out of the blue and led me to a group. Helene's God story included a truly miraculous encounter. I have known many people who have had supernatural experiences from God, and their stories always amaze me. But I have known many more who, instead, have met God in much more mundane ways, ways that spoke to their spirit as certainly as God's amazing presence spoke to Helene: a phone call, a radio program, or a book that was the exact answer to a prayer. Or maybe it was a friend talking about God right when the seeker was thinking more about God; or words from a stranger that were exactly what the person needed to hear. On and on the list could go. The answers came after they had asked and at the right time.

But the bottom line is that if you seek him, he will show up. That is the first secret. And the good news is that he is already looking for you.

KEEP ON SEEKING

If you do not know him, then just seek him. Whenever we seek him, we are responding to his stirring something in us. So respond to that little voice inside, those thoughts, those wonderings. Talk to him; tell him that you are looking for him. Talk to someone who can help you.

If you do know him and cannot find him right now, hear this: that is normal too. Even if you feel that you are going through a "desert" experience and that God seems far, far away, know that in reality he is always near. Either there is some reason he is not doing anything at that moment, or he is doing something and you cannot see it. Though it may be distressing, it is a normal part of the spiritual life. The psalms are full of writings from people who felt that way:

> *Hurry with your answer, GOD!*
> *I'm nearly at the end of my rope.*
> *Don't turn away; don't ignore me!*
> *That would be certain death.*[1]

It is okay and normal to experience times like that, but the answer is always the same. It is the same "secret" . . . *seek*. Even when it seems he is not there, we can *trust* that he has not forsaken us. Remember what the psalmist said:

> *Those who know your name will trust in you,*
> *for you, LORD, have never forsaken those who seek you.*[2]

Whether you don't yet know him or already have some relationship with him and want to know him better, look at the verse below and see that God *wants* you to seek him. And when you do, he promises that he will reward your seeking.

> *It is impossible to please God without faith.*
> *Anyone who wants to come to him*
> *must believe that God exists and that he*
> *rewards those who sincerely seek him.*[3]

You do not have to have the biggest faith, or belief, in the world. Just the act of believing enough to *seek* is enough for him to come to you. Seek and you shall find.[4]

To live out this secret means that you will, first, *take a step from your heart.* So go to a quiet place and tell him you are looking for him. Pour out your heart. Ask Jesus to meet you and come to you. Ask him to show up in your life.

Second, you might want to *do this with someone else who knows him well.* Get with that person and pray together. If you have never done that, it may seem strange, but you will find it one of the most incredible spiritual experiences you can have. Ask him how he found God and what God does in his life.

Third, *seek him by reading the Bible*. He will talk to you there. It is his love letter to you. Forget your preconceptions, and just go there. If you have never read the Bible, begin in the psalms and the book of John. Talk to God about what you are reading, and sit still and let him talk to you.

Next, *seek him for the answers you need in your life*. Relationships, finances, troubles, guidance, kids, or whatever you need help with.

Seek and you will find.

*O*pening yourself up to the gifts of God means trusting that he loves you and will provide for you. It means daring to be vulnerable with both God and the right people. It often means trusting beyond what you can see. It means believing in the character of God even more than you believe in your desired outcome.

God's blessings await you. You hold the key that unlocks them: trust.

the *Key to All Other Secrets*

Trust Is the Key That Opens the Door to Blessings

Trust in the LORD with all your heart;
do not depend on your own understanding.
Seek his will in all you do,
and he will show you which path to take.

—PROVERBS 3:5–6 NLT

The act of trust, or faith, is the way we join ourselves to the sources of what we need. Since we are finite and limited, we have to get what we need from outside ourselves. From the beginning of life, we grow to the extent that we can trust and receive the things we need. The more we trust and invest in the sources that provide what we need, the more we will receive them.

This secret of trust is the key that opens the door to all the other secrets. Through trust, we connect with God in a way that shows our reliance on him and our surrender to him. This is what he desires most from us. He wants us to trust him and depend on him more than any other thing. In fact, he says that without trust, or faith, it is impossible to please him, to have a relationship with him, or to receive anything from him.[1] Trust is the essence of "faith," and it opens you up to all that you need from God.

Learning to depend on God will make your life larger than you could ever imagine and better, in every way. As you trust, you will step out in faith and receive blessings you never would have received and accomplish things you never thought possible. It is the way that your life becomes larger.

Rhonda Byrnes in *The Secret* says, "Your job is not to figure out the how. The how will show up out of a commitment and belief in the what."[2] I have to admire the strength of commitment and the willingness to believe in something beyond ourselves that I hear in this statement. As a Christian, the object of my faith—the what— is not an impersonal universe but a personal God. And when that willingness to believe—that trust—is placed in the God who really can help us, our lives will change in ever-expanding ways.

When I first set out on my faith path, I had no idea what it meant to trust God, but I found one of my first clues from a poster in a bookstore. It was a picture of an incredible sunset over an ocean, with this quote by Ralph Waldo Emerson:

All I have seen teaches me to trust the Creator
for all I have not seen.

It helped me over the initial hurdle of just trusting that God was there and that he knew what he was doing. After all, that amazing beauty did not come from nowhere. Someone created it. Someone a lot bigger and smarter than I. So, like Emerson said, I surmised that if he could create what I saw, he could probably take care of me.

And though I didn't have a clue what it all meant, I also remembered the verse from that initial day in my dorm room that said if God takes care of the birds of the air, then he can take care of me. Now, many years later, I am still blown away by this truth—and to think I almost missed it.

UNLOCKING THE SECRET OF TRUST

So how do we unlock the secret of trust? The first answer is that we take that very first step of faith. Like the Nike commercial says, we just do it.

Take That First Step of Faith

After my first "introduction" to God in college, I began trusting him to lead me and show me what I was supposed to do with my life. The real reason I had gone to college was to play college golf. I was an accounting and finance major; I had thought about law school and business but had no real goals and certainly no plan. But

31

my new "friends with faith" told me to ask God about my future and to "trust" him with it. Not really knowing what that meant, I asked anyway. Slowly, but in an unmistakable way, God began to lead me away from my secure accounting and finance major and into the field of psychology, which would render me basically un-employable after college, unless I went to graduate school. Though

MY LIFE HAS
GOTTEN LARGER
EVER SINCE
THOSE FIRST STEPS
OF FAITH.

I had taken no psychology classes and had no background there, God's mes-sage was clear. It took a great deal of trust, but I took the step of faith and changed my major.

Now, I'm not suggesting that you go out on unresearched or uncon-firmed limbs and saw them off from underneath you. I did a *lot* of research, verifying my aptitudes, gifts, and abilities before launch-ing very far into this new field. I had to find out if I was even qualified, and I did my due diligence. Even so, it was a leap of faith into the unknown.

But changing my major wasn't all God had in store for me; choosing a grad school became another lesson in faith. I had been accepted into a reputable school, Baylor University, near Dallas, where I was living at the time. I even had a job lined up with a clinic and an offer to become a partner after some training. Everything was so secure . . . no risk, no financial problems, no job hunting. Seemed like my step of faith to change my major was paying off and had brought me to a place of security. Until . . . I got a call from a program I had applied to in Los Angeles—a program that also taught theology as part of the training. One of their reps was coming through Dallas and wanted to set up an interview. There was no way I was going to move to Los Angeles. I didn't know anyone out there, and that place was weird anyway. I already had everything in place in Dallas . . . no way. But hey, what's an interview? Might be interesting just to meet the guy.

But as we chatted, something began to happen. I didn't hear a voice, but I did hear a direction. It was somewhere between a command and an awareness, and I knew it wasn't coming from me. It was basically a message: "Go to California." It was God telling me to leave all my security and step into nothingness and just trust him. There was no mistake about it. Somehow in that one-hour interview, I was told to go to Los Angeles and enroll in graduate school. No friends, no job, no future that I knew of—just God. So I took that first step, and I went. And my life has gotten larger ever since—all from those first steps of faith.

Just Jump

When my four-year-old was learning to swim, it was all I could do to get her to jump off the safety of the steps into my arms and let me pull her to the next level. "No, Daddy, what if I go under!"

I would coax and coax . . . "I won't let you go under. I promise. Trust me." After many, many episodes of that dance, she finally jumped off, grabbed my hands, and began to kick. Only then did she learn the magic of weightlessness: trusting me first, then trusting that it would all work.

How many times does God coax us to take that step . . . "Come on, I'm right here. I won't let you fall. I promise. Trust me." But we protest that we're afraid, we're worried that if we jump in, we'll go under, that he won't catch us. And all the while, just beyond the safety and security of where we are, he holds out joy and wonder and the larger life.

We don't always know what's in front of us or what will happen next; but if we know the One who knows, we can trust him to take care of things because we know he loves us. When I was making my decision to pull up stakes and move to California— even though I knew no one and had no idea what lay ahead of me when I got there—God showed me a scripture that really helped. It's about a man who lived a couple of thousand years ago who obeyed God's call to get up and move to an unknown place:

> *It was by faith that Abraham obeyed when God*
> *called him to leave home and go to another land*
> *that God would give him as his inheritance.*
> *He went without knowing where he was going.*[3]

I decided that if Abraham could do it, so could I. What I found when I got to California was that God had led me to a school of learning and development that was exactly what I needed to realize the career he had planned for me. He led me to a healing community that was exactly what I needed to become a person who could pull off that career. That same community offered me the healing I needed to become emotionally healthy and develop the relationships I desired in life.

He led me to each new step in my work, and he opened the door for every new opportunity. Each step of the way, he gave me the resources and the people I needed to fulfill that step. He provided each step, but each step required one thing from me as well: *trust*. I had to step out. And I have come to learn why he requires trust: trust moves us beyond where we are and connects us with what he wants to do for us and what he wants us to do for him.

Dare to Be Vulnerable

If we do not trust, we are limited to our own resources, and we weren't created to do it all on our own. When a baby enters the world, he or she has no choice but to trust its caretakers. And through the process of trust, the baby is cared for and nurtured and thrives. The baby gains weight and achieves mobility; its brain and body develop. He or she gets what's needed from outside itself by being vulnerable to the ones who are the source of what's needed. The baby cannot get those things alone. But by needing and trusting others, he or she thrives. We are the same.

A man once told me that he didn't trust *anyone*. I told him that was impossible and that he was in denial, but if it made him feel better to think that he was that insulated and independent, more power to him.

Then I asked him, "Did you drive here today? If you did, you trusted hundreds of people on the road headed right at you. Did you eat today? If so, you trusted that all those who prepared your food did not pass *E. coli* to you. Have you ever flown? When you fly, you trust the pilot not to be on crack cocaine that day. So don't tell me you don't trust anyone."

His real problem was that he was having difficulty trusting God to be there when he took a risk for his next growth step. But as he began to understand that he actually did trust strangers in his life each and every day, he was able to take little steps of trust toward God as well. What step is God asking you to take that makes you vulnerable?

Start with What You Need

So, what do *you* need to trust God for? Well, pretty much everything, but most of all, the things that you are not able to provide for yourself. That is how you get a larger life than you have, and it's also how you serve him and fulfill his purposes for you. You begin in the areas that place your well-being in his hands. Look at the list below and see how many of these experiences you've already gone through. Did you go through them with God, or did you try to go it alone? Next time, let him help you with your needs:

- Trust him to be there if you take a career step.
- Trust him to save your marriage.
- Trust him to help you learn to love again.
- Trust him to help you learn a skill that is needed for what he has asked you to do or that is needed to accomplish your dream.
- Trust him to provide the money you need to do what he has asked you to do.
- Trust him with your business.
- Trust him with your children.
- Trust him to take you through an illness when you get bad news.
- Trust him to help you through a breakup.
- Trust him with your future and give up worry.
- Trust him to help you overcome an emotional problem or addiction that you have not been facing.
- Trust him to go into counseling.
- Trust him to lead you to the help you need in some area of life.
- Trust him to help you find a community of faith or a community of healthy friends.
- Trust him to help you develop a dating life.

It's not trust if we have no need. Take a step. Jump in. Dare to believe. God will not let you down.

Trust God's Character, Not Any Particular Outcome

We've talked about some good outcomes of stepping out in faith and trust. We've seen how things sometimes work out well—very well. But what about the times when they don't? What then? Does this mean that God has let you down?

The Bible is very clear about this: we do not trust God based on particular outcomes we can see. Our trust is based on his love for us and his character. In fact, the Bible's faith chapter, Hebrews 11, gives us examples of people who stepped out in faith and endured horrific atrocities without ever receiving all that they were promised. Their reward would come later, but God was pleased by their faith.

It's easy to believe God on the mountaintop; but when we're in the valley and it's dark and we feel all alone, that's when our faith is tested. When we lose a loved one or a job, our health or a relationship, these are the times when trusting God is difficult. But they are also the times when we need him the most. They are the times when we need to know that no matter how bad it is, God is there with us, that he loves us and is going to take us through whatever we face.

If we keep holding on to God during the dark times, we will find that he never leaves our side as we walk through the pain and that when we come out on the other side, he is still there beside us and that our faith has been strengthened in the process. And so the next time we encounter difficulty, we are stronger and our trust in him is even greater. Sometimes he does not deliver us from our difficulty at all, but simply gives us his presence and the presence of others.

Trusting God through the bad times is the deepest kind of faith there is. It is the kind that Jesus modeled for us when he faced death and cried out, "My God, my God, why have you forsaken me?"[4] It is the kind that Job had when he lost everything and said, "Though he slay me, yet will I trust in him."[5] Like Job, those who

TRUSTING GOD THROUGH THE BAD TIMES IS THE DEEPEST KIND OF FAITH THERE IS.

have known God for years have come to a place where no matter what happens, they trust the One who loved them enough to die for them, because they know his character.

They know he is the only and true God, that he is a good God, and that he loves us enough to die for us. So, when we have that kind of faith, even when we don't understand it all, we know enough to trust God based on his love for us and his character.

Trust God Even When You Don't Understand

I recently had a wonderful experience that began with a casual conversation and ended with someone beginning a relationship with God. I was talking with a hotel staff person on a trip, and when she found out that I wrote books on psychology and the spiritual life, she said, "Oh, I just had an experience that made me think about all of that."

"What was that?"

"A friend of mine died in the prime of life. He was a wonderful man, great husband and father, but he had a very fast-growing cancer and died. It was so heartbreaking, especially as I thought about his family. I knew him through work and did not know his family, so I was feeling very bad for them and his other friends whom I did not know. I was devastated.

"But when I went to the funeral, pretty heartbroken myself over this tragedy, it was much different than I had expected," she said.

"How was that?" I asked.

"Well, instead of being so gloomy, it was more like a celebration. It was so different."

"Celebration?"

"Yeah," she continued. "He and his family were believers in God and heaven, and they were all talking mostly about where he is now and how they knew they would all see him again. I mean they were sad and stuff, like they miss him . . . but they were okay in another way. It was like they really, truly believed they would be with him again."

"I am sure they will," I said.

"How can you be sure of that?" she asked. "I mean, do you believe that?"

"I know that this may sound strange," I said, "but at this point in my life, I would not even say 'believe.' I would say I 'know' they will."

"How can you know?" she asked.

"Because Jesus said he would take anyone who believed in him with him to heaven. And I know that Jesus is still alive today, because I have seen him do so much over the years. I know him," I said. "So when someone dies, we can know that we will see him again, in a very real place just like now. And that is why the Bible says that as believers, we do not 'grieve like people who have no hope.'[6] We are sad, but we are certain that it is not over."

"Don't you ever have doubts?" she asked.

"I used to," I said. "But now, I don't doubt that he is real. I have just seen too much. Mind you, there is a lot I don't understand, especially when bad things happen, like your friend's death. But I know he is real, and I trust him with the things I do not understand and take comfort in the fact that he gets it even when I don't.

"It's kind of how it is with my daughters, who are five and six. There are things that happen that I totally understand, but they don't. When they ask me about them, I explain them, but they still can't get it. They are not yet capable of understanding some of the things that adults can fully comprehend. So they just nod, let it go, and ask, 'What's for dinner?' Somehow they are okay with the fact that they don't get it and I do. Likewise, I don't have a problem with the fact that there are things I do not understand about God or why he allows some things to happen.

If I can understand things my kids can't, I can certainly see how an infinite God can understand things that I can't. Besides, how could I expect to fully comprehend an infinite God? Who would even want a God who we could be as smart as? He would be a pretty useless God if he were no smarter than a human."

WHEN WE CONNECT OURSELVES TO THE SOURCE OF ALL THAT'S GOOD, WE OPEN OUR LIVES UP TO UNIMAGINABLE BLESSINGS.

We went on to talk more about how to begin a relationship with him, and she did, right then and there. It was an awesome experience, and it made me reflect on the truth and the power of this secret of God: when we connect ourselves to the source of all that's good—even when we don't quite understand it all—we open our lives up to unimaginable blessings.

Don't Step Out into Stupidity

I cringe every time I hear one of those stories of a parent taking a child off medication and "stepping out in faith" to trust God to heal him or her, only to meet with disastrous results. I feel sorry for people who naively lose all they own by taking some foolish leap of faith and gambling everything on a crazy business venture. I feel sad when people quickly marry someone they hardly know, saying they were going to trust God to make it work. Trust is not the same thing as stupidity.

Satan once tried to get Jesus to just jump off a cliff and trust God to catch him. Jesus responded to him by saying that we should not test God.[7] God is not responsible for our idiotic decisions and will not bail us out when we make them. He gave us brains to use. Trust is stepping out in faith that God will do what he has said he will do or has clearly directed us to do. He can be trusted to keep his promises. But we cannot presume that he will sign off on everything we want him to do and just blindly go ahead. Don't confuse foolishness with faith.

MOVING INTO THE LARGER LIFE

So, where are you in trusting God? Is there some area of life that you need for him to make larger or better? Can you trust him to do that? Here are a few tips for living it out.

Know Who It Is You Are Trusting

Read the Bible and learn about God's character. The more you know about him, the easier it will be to trust him. You might enjoy reading the psalms; chapter after chapter reveals attributes and characteristics of God. They will remind you of who you are dealing with.

You'll also want to get to know Jesus, for Jesus said that if we have seen him, we have seen the Father.[8] Look at the pages of the Gospels and see Jesus's love, his care, his compassion, and his power. That is who you are trusting. Watch him as he deals with his sheep, and remember that you *are* one.

Decide What Needs to Change, and Define the Steps

Look at the areas of life that you want to be different, and ask yourself how much faith you are exercising in those areas. Ask God to help you make clear decisions about what you want to change, and then define the steps of trust you must take to make that change happen. Remember, faith without action is dead.[9] If you are not stepping out in some way that is vulnerable, you are not being stretched and are not growing in your faith. What first step do you need to take? Your first step may not be a cakewalk, but God will always be there to catch you if you fall, and he will always have your best interests in mind. Define the steps of trust and faith that you want to take and take them.

Rewrite Your "Trust Map" If Necessary

Ask yourself if there was anything from your past that has harmed your ability to trust. Was it people? The church? Did you have a traumatic experience? All of those can affect our ability to trust and make us be like the man earlier in the chapter who said he didn't trust anyone. We all can imagine what his past probably looks like. Find out where you got your "trust map" and begin to rewrite the path of your future. If necessary, get some counseling to help.

Share in the Faith Testimonies of Others

Read about others' faith stories and hear their testimonies. The Bible says that seeing what others have done and what God has done in their lives helps our own faith. Do an Internet search on testimonies of Christians or other research. You will be amazed at what God is doing around the world.

Trust is a muscle that can grow as you learn to be certain that he can bring about what you cannot see. Of course you can't see it yet! It will only come into being as you take that step, the step of trust.

TRUSTING HIS PERSON AND HIS WAYS

Up until this point, our insights into *the secret things of God* have centered upon God himself and our relationship to him. Now we're going to take a bit of a turn. We'll spend the next few sections looking at some of the secrets God has given us so that it might go well with us[10] in the areas of life that matter to us most: our emotional well-being, our relationships, and our purpose. We will find that the Creator himself has told us how to make the life he created work best.

The final section of this story will bring us full circle, back to some *unreligious* secret things of God that will ground you and prepare you to live out all the secrets you've discovered in this book.

Let's go unlock some treasure.

God created us with the capacity and the desire to feel happy. We all want that sometimes elusive sense of well-being that makes us feel that all is right in our world. And while being happy is not God's only or even highest priority for us, he very much wants us to have a sense of well-being—he wants us to be filled with joy and peace and hope. Like so much else in this world, there are laws and principles that govern our happiness.

As you'll see in the next few pages, those spiritual principles can transform your life.

Secrets about Happiness

There Is No Such Thing as Disconnected and Happy

If one falls down, his friend can help him up.
But pity the man who falls and has no one to help him up!
—Ecclesiastes 4:10 NIV

Dave was a successful entrepreneur and everyone's favorite. With his outgoing personality, you would think he had it all: friends, more than enough money, a beautiful family, and the world by the tail. Until . . .

A change in the market began to bring some stress on his manufacturing business. It was nothing that couldn't be solved, and though it was stressful, it should not have been a long-term threat. A few articles appeared in the business section of the newspapers about the company's difficulty and future, which is typical when this kind of downturn occurs. But all in all, nothing happened that an executive at his level shouldn't be able to handle. That is what they do. But for some reason it started to get to him. The fact that the public viewed him as less than successful, plus the stress of the financial consequences, began to take its toll.

Slowly he began to withdraw. He pulled back from seeing his friends, playing golf, going to church, and hanging out. He stayed at the office later and later, "working it all out," he told his wife. What no one realized was that he was unplugging from the people who cared about him most. And without anyone realizing it, it got a lot worse.

Finally he went MIA. One day he just didn't show up for work. Then he didn't show up the next day . . . or the next. No one could find him, including his board. They eventually found him locked up in the hotel suite where he had been staying for weeks. His wife thought he had been on an extended business trip. His board called me to help and brought him to my office—they came along to make sure he didn't back out. What had happened? He had slowly gone into a deep depression and could not get out of it. The stress of it all, as he put it, had "done him in."

"So . . . how did you get to this place?" I asked.

"I don't know," he said. "I don't know. It's not like me, really. I'm a pretty up person. But this thing, I guess, has just been too hard. I don't know what happened."

"Who were you talking to during all of this?" I asked.

"Everyone!" he said. "The banks, the partners, the markets . . . I had to talk to all of them."

"No, no, no," I said. "I mean, who were you talking to about how you were feeling and doing with it all? Who were you unloading and decompressing with?"

"Unloading what?"

"How depressed and scared you were? Obviously that is what did you in."

"I don't know what you mean," he said. "I didn't want to bother anyone with all that. It was my problem . . . I just needed to figure it all out and solve it. I thought I could, but it got to be too much. It did me in. I couldn't take it anymore. I just had to get away."

"You know what?" I said. "I don't think your business problems are what 'did you in,' as you say. You're smart enough to fix those. I think what did you in is something else."

"What?"

"What did you in was the 'getting away.' Not just taking a break from work and the stress. What I mean is that when things got hard, you tried to do it on your own, without the support of other people. That is what I think. We have to find out why you chose to handle this on your own—why you chose to disconnect from the people you needed the most at a time you needed them most."

"I have no clue what you're talking about . . ." His voice drifted off as he stared right through me. I knew at that moment why it had all gone down the drain and also that we had a lot of work to do.

Dave's crash and the loss of his business, which he did lose because he went MIA, had nothing to do with business. His business problems were solvable. His crash and his business loss actually came from not knowing one of the most important secrets of God: we are not meant to be alone.

YOUR LIFE DEPENDS ON IT!

Hear this: in order for life to work, it must be lived in the way it was designed. And it was designed by God to be lived in close relationship with others. Not only your happiness but your very life depends on your ability to connect with others in a deep and meaningful way. God made you that way, because he is that way. If only Dave had known this ancient secret from Ecclesiastes:

> Two are better than one,
> because they have a good return for their work. . . .
> Though one may be overpowered,
> two can defend themselves.
> A cord of three strands is not quickly broken.[1]

God did not intend for us to be alone. One of the secrets of our faith is that our God, who made us in his image, is not isolated. He does not exist "by himself." He exists in relationship and always has. The Father, the Son, and the Spirit are all one, but they are also separate persons who exist in love with one another. Haven't you noticed that everything in the universe that is alive is relational in nature? Rocks aren't alive and they aren't relational; but puppies are. The things that have *breath* are all in relationship to others. We live in a relational universe. To survive, and to prosper, we have to be connected to others.

WE ARE NOT MEANT TO BE ALONE.

One of the Bible's words for this is the Greek word *koinonia*. It is often translated "fellowship" but means much more. Probably if you asked Dave if he had "fellowship" in his life, he would have said yes. He had "friends," like business associates and golfing buddies. But that is not what the Bible is talking about with this word. It's talking about relationships that go deeper than the surface, to a place where our hearts are literally connected to one another in the spiritual realm. When we have this kind of fellowship, as Paul refers to it, our hearts are "knit together in love"[2] and we become "one in spirit."[3] The word *koinonia* does not mean "Jell-O and crummy casseroles in the fellowship hall of some church basement," but things like "sharing" and "oneness," where your whole life is "knit together" with others. It means that whatever you go through, others are partaking of that experience with you and helping to metabolize it.

Just think if Dave had had what King David had with his friend Jonathan when he was going through his horrible stress:

51

After David had finished talking with Saul,
Jonathan became one in spirit with David,
and he loved him as himself.[4]

What would have happened? Dave would have handled things totally differently; his talents, brains, creativity, and energy would have come to bear fully on the problem, and his company would have been saved, just like King David's kingdom was saved.

THE RESEARCH IS IN

This is not theory. It is the secret of God's design, and it is also in the research. There is more data on this reality than almost anything in health psychology. People who are connected to others have been shown to have better brain development and immune systems and less psychological vulnerability to all sorts of problems like depression, anxiety, addictions, and the like. They have higher resiliency in illness, fewer heart problems, cancer, strokes, arthritis, etc., etc., etc. The list just goes on and on. In other words, the more connected you are, the happier and healthier you are.

Why? Because you were designed to be like God, in deep loving relationships all the days of your life. It goes "from the womb to the tomb." Babies and old people are healthy only when they are close to others. Not only healthier, but they think better as well. Being connected to others affects stress response and stress-hormone-release levels in the brain. When someone has too many stress hormones flowing, thinking gets impaired. Dave could have used some help in that regard.

One of my favorite examples of connectedness comes from a body of research regarding cortisol release in monkeys, rats, and other animals under stress. Cortisol is not something you want a great deal of floating around in your brain. It is a strong stress hormone. When they put a monkey in a cage and pipe in loud, scary noises (thus, high stress for the poor monkey), the amounts of this chemical in the monkey's system is—as you'd expect—very high. But get this . . . when they put one of his buddies in the cage with him—even though the loud, scary noises are continued—*the amount of cortisol in his brain goes down*. The outside stressor is the same, but the inside stress level goes down just from having a friend nearby.

Do not think that just because you're not a hermit in a cave that you're not isolated. You will be happy to the degree that you let others in. You have to learn to open up with a few people. You can do this by getting into a support group, a Bible-study group where sharing goes on, or a prayer group. You can meet for coffee with a few close friends, gather with a group who process life together, or meet with a therapist. The form of the outlet is not important. The question is, will you let others get close? Let others in, and you will be happier in the long haul. The words Barbra Streisand sang are true, "People who need people are the luckiest people in the world."

YOUR THOUGHTS AFFECT THE WAY YOU FEEL

Bad news won't bother them;
they have decided to trust the LORD.
—PSALM 112:7 CEV

What happens inside your head will find its way outside—into your life.

One of the things I like about Rhonda Byrne's book *The Secret* is the emphasis it puts on the power of our thoughts. Although I don't agree that we can attract everything we want to ourselves through our thoughts, as if we were God. I do appreciate Byrne's emphasis on the impact our thoughts have on our lives and our ability to control them. Our thoughts are so important to our well-being and to the outcomes of life that the Bible talks about them a lot.[5]

Many of us feel powerless to control our thoughts, but being in control of our thoughts is one of the secrets to controlling how we feel—and thus, how *happy* we are. The apostle Paul tells us to "take captive every thought to make it obedient to Christ."[6] In other words, you don't need to let stuff roll around in your head that is not of God; that kind of negativity does not produce

Secrets about Happiness

life. Anything that destroys good things in you is not from God. Listen to how *The Message* paraphrases the apostle Paul's words:

> We use our powerful God-tools for smashing warped philosophies,
> tearing down barriers erected against the truth of God,
> fitting every loose thought and emotion and impulse
> into the structure of life shaped by Christ.[7]

I love that phrase "fitting every loose *thought* and *emotion* and *impulse* into the structure of life shaped by Christ." Do you have a few of those loose thoughts and emotions and impulses running around inside your head? When those "warped" thoughts shoot through your head, they can control your life, your relationships, and your destiny. They can make you depressed, despondent, hopeless, addicted, or anxious. They can also ruin your relational life and your ability to meet your goals and dreams. It's imperative that you gain control of what goes on inside your head. Because the truth is, *what happens inside your head will find its way outside—into your life.*

RESEARCH PROVES IT

We know this is true because "the Bible tells us so," as the nursery song goes. But research also confirms that your thoughts have a huge impact on your life. Optimism research has shown that thinking affects all the important areas of life. The same research shows that negative thinking also affects your life, as researcher Martin Seligman has learned after years of observation. Through his research, Seligman learned that there are three characteristically negative ways some people interpret, or explain, the things that happen in their lives.[8]

The first one is *personal* explanations. In this way of thinking, if something difficult happens, it's because there's something "wrong" with you, something personal. Let's say you call on customers, and they don't buy your product. If you walk away thinking, *They think I am an idiot. I am such a loser. I can't sell anything,* then you have personalized the event to mean something bad about yourself, rather than simply observing, *I guess they just don't need what I am selling today.*

The second one is *pervasive* explanations. This is where you interpret one difficulty as being pervasive across all of your life. Instead of this being about one sales call, you begin to think, *Not only can I not sell, the rest of my life is in the toilet too. Nothing I try to do goes right. I screw up everything.* This sense of pervasive failure sets you up for future failure and is a ticket to depression and misery.

The third interpretation is when you see one incident as proving a *permanent* quality about your life. This viewpoint can make everything seem hopeless, and you begin to feel helpless. *Not only did I not make this sale, this is how it will always be. No one will ever buy anything from me.* Whenever we think that "one bad time" is going to be "for all time," we are in trouble.

You have a choice to make here. You can be in control and take your thoughts captive, or you can let them tie you up in knots and lead you down all kinds of screwy paths. I'm going to give you some verbal rebuttals you can use to smash those warped philosophies and tear down the barriers erected against God's truth.[9] Ready? Here we go.

SMASH THAT DESTRUCTIVE THINKING

When you run up against a bump in the road—or even if you run into something more like a hurricane—God has given you the power to take your thinking patterns "captive to the obedience of Christ."[10] You can rebut them by using the powerful "God-tools" and reminding yourself of God's truth:

1. "I am not a loser. I am child of God, and he loves me and is going to help me in every way" (combats the *personal* mis-explanations).

   I am convinced that nothing can ever separate us from God's love.
   Neither death nor life, neither angels nor demons,
   neither our fears for today nor our worries about tomorrow—
   not even the powers of hell can separate us from God's love.
   No power in the sky above or in the earth below—
   indeed, nothing in all creation will ever be able to separate us
   from the love of God that is revealed in Christ Jesus our Lord.[11]

2. "This event is not going to be true for every area of my life, for God is in ultimate control and will bring good out

of everything that happens" (combats the *pervasive* mis-explanations).

> *We know that God causes everything to work together*
> *for the good of those who love God*
> *and are called according to his purpose for them.*[12]

3. "My future is not bleak, and life will not always be this way. God will never leave me or forsake me. There is no such thing as a hopeless future with God in the picture" (combats the *permanent* mis-explanations).

> *God has said, "Never will I leave you;*
> *never will I forsake you."*[13]

> *There is surely a future hope for you,*
> *and your hope will not be cut off.*[14]

This kind of thinking is guaranteed to help you move toward a sense of well-being, and research proves it. And the nice thing about it is that the power doesn't have to come from you. Every one of these "rebuttals" points to God as the power source. Your job is to make the choice to plug into it and to *take your thoughts captive.*

NO FEAR OF BAD NEWS

Just the other day, while writing this book, I got some bad news on a project I am involved in. Some issues with the partners in the venture were not going well, and it was very discouraging, especially financially. It was also somewhat scary, as there were some significant consequences for me. I instantly felt the blow emotionally. But, just as quickly, this verse came to mind:

> *He will have no fear of bad news;*
> *his heart is steadfast, trusting in the LORD.*[15]

When that verse came to mind, it immediately affected my thinking about the incident. I could feel my heart settle down. God's truth was having its way over my feelings and my thoughts. And, as the monkey research shows, when I called other people to help me work on the problem, I was much more calm and had better judgment, because I was no longer alone in the situation. I imagine that the cortisol 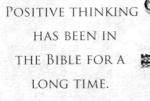 POSITIVE THINKING HAS BEEN IN THE BIBLE FOR A LONG TIME. levels in my brain went way down! At least I was somewhat sane, thanks to God's truth. Positive thinking is not some New Age fantasy. It has been in the Bible for a long time.

You have more control over how you feel than you may realize. Again we see that research backs up what life and the Bible tells us. The research of psychiatrist Aaron Beck[16] has shown that some emotional problems are clearly linked to negative thinking, usually about three areas: *the world, ourselves,* and *our future.* The way you view these areas has a huge effect on your happiness.

59

How do you see the world? Do you see it as a scary place where only bad things happen? Remember the story of Dave? That's what he did. He saw the world as a place where you would not be loved if you were failing. *My friends don't want to hear about this stuff*, he thought. So he isolated. And the result of this thinking was disaster.

I have seen singles, for example, stay alone and not work on their dating lives because of the way they see the world. They think, *There are no good ones out there. All the good ones are already taken,* and so they don't try. All the while, other more positive people are getting dates with the "good ones" who are supposedly all gone! The same thing happens with jobs, customers, deals, churches, and everything else "out there." If you see the world as a place God has created for you, that has good things in it for you, you will find, as the Bible says, the "desires of your heart"[17] accomplished and your "longings fulfilled." And as Proverbs says, that will be "sweet to the soul."[18]

But if you think the world is all bad and corrupt with no good opportunities left for you, you won't even go outside, like this "loafer" in Proverbs:

> Loafers say, "It's dangerous out there!
> Tigers are prowling the streets!"
> and then pull the covers back over their heads.[19]

As a result of his negativity, the guy in this verse never leaves his house and never finds anything good.

How you think about *yourself* and your *future*, Beck says, can also affect you in negative ways. As we saw in Seligman's research, negative outlooks in those areas will put you in emotional prison. But you have the "get out of jail free" card. You have the ability to capture your thoughts and maintain your freedom.

TURN YOUR HEAD AROUND

How do you turn your head—and your life—around? You start by *monitoring* your thoughts—supervising them, screening them, keeping an eye on them—like parents do their children. You do it by watching yourself for "catastrophizing" interpretations of events or potential future events. These are the "awfulizing" ways we talk to ourselves. You know what I'm talking about. Something happens, or we think something might happen, and we think, *Oh, man! There's no way I can deal with this! I am awful. This is horrible*, or *My world will end if this happens. That would be terrible. I could not stand it!* Such thinking leads to horrible depression and/or anxiety.

In reality, the things you dread may be hard or difficult, but your world *won't* end, you *can* deal, and you *can* make it through. But if you think about those things in depressing and catastrophic ways, then they become self-fulfilling prophecies, and as a result, you do not function well enough to deal with them.

Take some time to figure out where you got those views of yourself or the world or the future. You may have very good reasons to think the way you do. For example, you may see yourself negatively because of some people in your past. If you grew up with criticism, then you will have criticism in your head until you chase it out and replace it with good people's voices. Or you may see life the way you do because you experienced some horrible abuse or trauma in the past, and that has affected how you think at very deep levels. Figuring out *why* you think the way you do is an important step to change.

Here's a list of ways to understand and change your thinking:

- *Monitor* and observe it: take it captive to obedience.

- *Analyze* it: keep what's true and reject what's false.

- *Replace* what is false with God's truth.

- *Live out* the truth in faith, sometimes in spite of what you feel.

- *Get to the root* of those voices inside—where they came from and who they belong to.

- *Cut yourself loose* from the influence and power of the voices in your past.

- *Open up* to new people who love you and support you.

- *Internalize* these new messages of encouragement and validation that come from the positive people in your life. (The Bible has some great "one another" verses about how we're supposed to treat each other.[20])

- *Read* God's Word and other truth-giving and inspiring material.

- *Listen* to inspiring teachers and communicators.

- *Memorize* God's Word so it will be in your head all the time.

- *Gain* new experiences that disprove the old messages in your head.

Remember the story of Joshua and Caleb? They were sent by Moses, along with ten other men, to spy on the Promised Land and scope it out. The other ten came back saying, "No way can we capture that land. The enemies are too strong. Bad things will happen to us. We will never be able to do it! Let's not even try."

But Joshua and Caleb thought differently. They remembered the promises of God and said, "If God is with us, we can do it!"[21] As a result, the Promised Land was secured for the children of Israel for generations to come.

But as Seligman reminds us, *not all of them made it*. The pessimists, the negative thinkers, the ones who were ruled by their negative thoughts, did not make it to the Promised Land. For this secret held true: *their thinking became their reality*, as it does for all of us. You have the ability to turn your head around and take your thoughts captive. Your future may depend on it!

YOU ARE AS HAPPY AS YOU ARE FREE

Christ has set us free to live a free life.
So take your stand!
Never again let anyone put a harness of slavery on you.

—GALATIANS 5:1 *THE MESSAGE*

Slavery is one of the overriding metaphors in the Bible. It began when the children of Israel were held as slaves in Egypt under Pharaoh. In fact, it is the story God cites to explain the entirety of his law and purposes toward us. Moses told the Israelites that if they were asked what all of this "God stuff" (his rules and laws) was about, to simply say, "We were slaves . . . in Egypt, but the LORD brought us out . . . with a mighty hand."[22] If you lived then, that would be all the explanation you needed, for everyone knew that no one got out of Egypt without help. The fact that they got out proved that God is an awesome God.

LOSS OF CHOICE MEANS LOSS OF FREEDOM

Have you ever been a slave in Egypt? Probably not, if you are reading this book. But I'll bet you can identify with the idea of slavery somewhere in your life—and with the need for deliverance.

Secrets about Happiness

Slavery happens when you lose your freedom to *choose*, whether it relates to people or to patterns of behavior. Here are some of the ways I've heard people express their loss of freedom:

"We want to have some holidays at our own house and not go to my in-laws. I feel like our kids need some memories of just our family, but we always have to go to my husband's parents' house for every holiday. There is no way we could say we weren't coming."

"My mother won't take no for an answer. I have been trying to get some help for depression, so I started seeing a psychologist. It seems to be helping, but when I told her about it, she said she wants to come to the sessions with me. I told her that I need to go by myself, and that this is my therapy, but she is putting a lot of guilt on me to take her. I don't want to take her, but I feel like I should. How do I say no?"

"I know I need to break up with him, but when I do, I just get really sad and think of all the good times. So even though he is not good for me, and I don't like the way it is, I just miss him and love him too much. I keep going back every time we break up. *I can't not go back.* Then I do, and it is not good."

"I am tired of being controlled by food. I obsess about it when I go on a diet, and I obsess about it when I don't. It controls my head all the time, and also my behavior. I can't get free from it."

"I hate it after I look at porn on the Internet. I feel so bad about myself, and I'm afraid someone is going to find out. But I can't stop."

YOU WERE
CREATED
TO BE FREE.

"I don't know why I keep trying to earn my father's approval. I know I never can, but there is such a pull. I always think that this time he is going to be proud of something I do, but he isn't. He always finds something wrong or says how it could be better, and I am devastated."

"My boss is a jerk. He never appreciates anything I do, and I work harder than anyone around here. He just wants more and more, and the harder I work, the more he takes advantage of me. I feel like a slave."

Wherever there is a loss of freedom, there is a loss of happiness to some degree. Sometimes, to a large degree. "Learned helplessness" is one of the classic and most researched causes of depression and despair. It occurs when people feel as if they have no choices that will make a difference. When we don't have choices, we don't have freedom, and we get depressed.

This secret of God tells us what research has confirmed: you were created to be free. God does not want anyone or any behavior to control you.

Now the Lord is Spirit, and where the Spirit of the Lord is,
there is freedom.[23]

He made you to be free, and that is the only way you will be happy. If there is an area of your life where you have lost your freedom, this secret says *"get it back."* And sometimes keeping that freedom means you have to take a proactive stand.

There are times when you have to just say no to whoever or whatever you feel is controlling you. And if you can't, then read on, and you'll see how to do that. But first, let's start with a list of things in your life where you may have lost control:

- a substance (alcohol, drugs, nicotine)
- food
- sex
- striving to perform
- striving to gain someone's approval
- striving to gain someone's love
- striving to gain someone's acceptance
- obsessed with a desire or goal
- obsessed with or out of control of money
- striving for power
- an inappropriate need for status
- allowing someone else's problems or addictions to control you

67

- allowing someone else's mean or dysfunctional behavior to control you

- controlled by fear

- controlled by guilt

The message is that God wants you to be free. And when the Bible talks about control, it talks about being controlled by the Spirit[24] and about *self*-control—not "other control." In fact, part of the "fruit of the Spirit" in the book of Galatians is self-control.[25] God wants you to be in control of the things he has given you. They are yours to control and give away as you choose, not as other people demand. Here are some things that are yours to control:

- time
- energy
- money
- resources
- talents

- brains
- beliefs
- values
- desires
- love

- body
- choices
- limits

No one should be in control of how you spend or give these things except you.

RECLAIMING YOUR GOD-GIVEN FREEDOM

Some of your loss of happiness may be coming from your loss of freedom. So put two and two together, and begin to work on the real problem. How? God has given us the plan:

Secrets about Happines

STOP the Things That Are in Your Control

Your first step is to "just say no!" Now, before you say, "Well if I could, I would, but I can't," listen for a moment. I understand that there are losses of freedom that you cannot control and truly have become captive to, like an addiction. We will get to those. But there are *some slaveries that are just voluntary.*

You do have the ability to walk away from these slaveries, but you are refusing to do so because *you love the object of your slavery more than you want to admit.* Yet whatever is controlling you is destroying you. Long-term, you know you have to walk away, so walk. Want an old-fashioned word for it? Obedience. Obey what you know is right, and good things will happen, and the destruction will stop:

> *Be careful to obey so that it may go well with you.*[26]

You cannot continue to do something that you know is destructive and expect things to go well. If you play with fire, you will get burned—no matter how positive your thinking is. So stop it. And the best way to find out if you can stop is to just stop. Whatever it is you need to do—*just do it.*

You've heard people say, "I just quit. Cold turkey," or, "I just decided he was no good for me, so I broke up with him," or, "I just got sick of it, so I quit." Sometimes when I ask my five-year-old why she did something she wasn't supposed to do and knew it, she will say, "No reason. I just wanted to!" So I tell her, "Then stop it."

69

If You Need Help, ADMIT IT

If you can't "just stop," admit it. Admit that you can't handle the situation on your own and that you are powerless over whoever or whatever is controlling you. Admit that you are an "addict" to whatever it is. That does not mean you're "bad," remember? (See the "Secrets about God" section concerning guilt.) It means that God understands that you are a slave in Egypt who can't get out alone, and he wants to help you. So just admit it. Stop rationalizing, minimizing, and excusing it by thinking you will stop sometime. You can't, so just admit it. Breaking free of addictions is not easy. So after you admit it, you need to do two more things.

1. Ask God for help. Reach out to God, and he will show up. Ask him for the power to find a way to escape and the strength to do it. You do not have the power, but he does. He promises that power to you, as well as a way out of whatever is controlling you:

I can do everything through him who gives me strength.[27]

*The temptations in your life are no different
from what others experience.
And God is faithful. He will not allow the temptation
to be more than you can stand.
When you are tempted, he will show you
a way out so that you can endure.*[28]

2. Ask other people for help. Like we saw with Dave earlier in this chapter, God created us to need other people. In addition to connecting with God, you've also got to reach out to others for love and strength. The Bible commands us to help each other when someone loses their freedom and gets caught up in something that will hurt them.[29]

I'm sure you've noticed that al-coholics usually do not get free until they join a recovery group, no matter

REACH OUT TO GOD, AND HE WILL SHOW UP.

how many times they promise themselves and others they will stop. You may have known a sex and romance addict who could not get free from a person or a behavior, or a codependent who could not get free from an addict—until she joined a group or saw a counselor.

If you're in a place where you need help, then you've got to go to a support group, and you have to go more than once. You have to go until you are truly free.

Figure Out the Source

Next you've got to figure out what's driving you to give up your freedom. There is always a need behind it. Maybe you're trying to make a *trade*. Were you hoping to trade your freedom for some-thing that would fill your emptiness? What emptiness are you try-ing to fill with that person or that behavior?

Or maybe there is a cover-up going on. What hurt are you trying to cover up by that behavior? What pain are you trying to medicate by that obsessive drive to have "that person"? Sometimes, to get free, you might have to do some soul work with a good counselor, a wise person, or a recovery group to get to the root of why you gave up your freedom. But once you do, you will solve it.

Choose Life

Give yourself to life-enhancing things. As you choose love and health and life, you will not need whatever it was that you were addicted to. Find good community and good support. Find your talents and put them to use. Give yourself to serving God and others. As you get into the good stuff, which is not addicting but fulfilling, you will rediscover your freedom from the things that enslaved you.

DEALING WITH NEGATIVE EMOTIONS LEADS TO HAPPY ONES

Sorrow is better than laughter,
because a sad face is good for the heart.
—ECCLESIASTES 7:3 NIV

It is a paradox, but sometimes to feel better, we have to feel worse.

My first job in the field of psychology was as a psychiatric aide in a psychiatric hospital. I took a year off between college and graduate school to make sure of my calling and that this was what I wanted to do for the rest of my life. It was invaluable experience. But I have to admit, in the beginning something surprised me.

I kind of thought that psychologists and psychiatrists were supposed to make depressed people feel better. So it made sense to me that that's what they would do in a hospital. But what I found was the opposite. It seemed that they *tried to make them feel worse!* In the group sessions, they would get people to talk about their hurts, their pain, their losses, the trauma of the divorce they just went through, the sadness of past abuse and trauma, their abandonments, anger, bitterness, and the like. Groups were not "happy talk" at all. They were the opposite—a lot of talk about a lot of pain and misery.

But I learned something. The secret that God revealed through Solomon in the verse above is true: a sad face is good for the heart.

It's true that sometimes we have to feel worse before we can feel better. We have to face the pain we are not dealing with in order to get past a depression or an addiction or whatever it is we are suffering with. Just waiting for the pain to go away is not enough. It may take a little surgery.

DRAIN THE WOUND

Just yesterday, a caller on the radio told me she was distressed because, as she said, "A year and a half after my divorce, and I am still spiraling downward. I get depressed and can't get out of it. I am still overcome with my feelings about it all." And then the clincher, "You would think that after a year and a half, I would be over this!"

Well, not necessarily. The saying "time heals all things" is just not true. If you have an infected finger, the last thing you want to do is give it more time. Untreated, it will get worse, and eventually you'll get gangrene and may even lose it. But if you open it up, drain it, clean it out, and put a little medicine in it, it will heal.

Our hearts, minds, and souls are exactly like that. When someone has hurt us—or we've allowed someone to hurt us—we need to drain that wound before we're going to get any relief. If we'll open it up and clean it out and put in a little medicine, it will get better. Just like cleaning out a wound, it hurts for a little bit, but in the long run, it's worth it. The statement, "Blessed are those who mourn, for they shall be comforted,"[30] is true at so many levels. We do not need to walk around with toxins inside of us, either physically or emotionally. They wear against our health and destroy everything we are trying to do. So we need to clean them out. If we don't, they'll infect our lives.

OLD HURTS, IF THEY ARE NOT HEALED, KEEP US FROM TRUSTING NEW RELATIONSHIPS.

Old hurts, for example, if they are not healed, keep us from trusting new relationships. The woman I mentioned earlier was not free to look at any new relationship because she had not gotten over the old one. Why? Not enough time? No, not really. A year and a half should be enough to at least get her off the bottom. The problem was (I found as I quizzed her further), she had never done the work of dealing with her pain. She had gone to six sessions of divorce recovery at her church and decided she did not like the group. She had tried some counseling but quit that also. She kept telling me she had read some books but that they had not done the job either.

I challenged her by saying that reading the books was good, but *doing what the books said was even more important*. I knew the books she was talking about and that they said to get into a process with safe, trustworthy people and deal with your hurt while receiving support and healing. If she did that, I told her, she would get over it. But not until.

So . . . hate to depress you, but this applies to you too. However, this really is good news. You do not have to be overcome by your pain. You just have to find a good place to deal with it. Find a safe friend, a group, or a recovery ministry. If necessary, put a support group together yourself and find some materials to guide you. If you need it, find a good professional counselor. Journaling your feelings might be a good outlet too. But be sure to deal with them in the context of relationship with others.

TAKE OUT THE TRASH

It would be nice if all we had to deal with in life was just our hurts. At least when we are hurt by others, we are innocent. We can receive empathy for how bad we had it, and we don't have to worry about anything from our side. Not that hurt is good, but at least it's not our fault. Unfortunately, that is not all there is to finding happiness. Not only do we have to drain the wounds, but we also have to take out the trash.

We all have crummy stuff inside of us that is not hurt, but our own darkness. Every religious, philosophical, or psychological system known to man has noticed the same thing: humans have a dark side. You can argue until doomsday about where it came from, but you can't escape that we have it. And as any good psychologist will tell you, if you don't deal with it, you will never be happy. And that is where God's secrets shine over and above any system of thought in the universe. God says it so simply, and yet his way is so effective: "Confess it, receive forgiveness for it, and move on." He wants us to be clean, so we have clean relationships that do not have all of that dysfunction that our darkness causes.

Now, really, do you want to look like an episode of *Jerry Springer*? At our worst moments, all of us could audition, at least for a scene or two. But that isn't how we want our relationships and lives to be, ruled by our darker feelings and motives. Envy, for example, ruins friendships. Jealousy divides marriages and families. Lust destroys lives, relationships, and chances of ever finding real fulfillment. Sarcasm drives people away. This darker side is played out every day on the *Springer* set. Don't let those things grow inside of you. Your heart is a garden, and it needs constant weeding. Here's what Jesus said about this secret:

> *It's what comes out of a person that pollutes:*
> *obscenities, lusts, thefts, murders, adulteries, greed, depravity,*
> *deceptive dealings, carousing, mean looks,*
> *slander, arrogance, foolishness—*
> *all these are vomit from the heart. There is the*
> *source of your pollution.*[31]

When we have thoughts and feelings like these, which we all do, we need to confess them to God and to someone else, and talk them out. As we do, we get cleansed. Listen to how John puts it:

If we are living in the light, as God is in the light,
then we have fellowship with each other,
and the blood of Jesus, his Son, cleanses us from all sin.
If we claim we have no sin, we are only fooling ourselves and
not living in the truth.
But if we confess our sins to him, he is faithful and just to
forgive us our sins
and to cleanse us from all wickedness.[32]

When we bring this crummy stuff out of the darkness and into the light with God and others, we get "purified." Don't feel bad! We all have feelings like those. They only become destructive if we don't deal with them and get them cleansed. If we don't deal with them, we end up projecting them onto others by judging them, fearing them, mistrusting them, controlling them, fighting with them, or some other dynamic. And if we don't do one of those, we end up acting out in some way.

The crummy things that we allow to grow inside could be nipped in the bud and weeded out if we just faced them and let God forgive and cleanse. We don't want to ignore them, on the one hand, and we don't want to act them out on the other. Instead, we need to talk them out and get free from them.

Whatever we do not bring into the light, whatever we keep in the darkness, ends up controlling us. That is why, for example, twelve-step groups are so effective in helping people overcome acting out. They deal with the dark stuff inside, in step four. The fearless moral inventory helps clean it all, and the light of forgiveness takes its place. And they do that on a regular basis. Good medicine, according to science and to God.

Here are some tips on how to do that:

1. Allow yourself to be aware of and observe your darker feelings and motives.

2. Agree with God and reality that these things are destructive.

3. Confess to God and to someone safe, and claim God's forgiveness. (It is yours; enjoy it.)

4. Ask God to remove these things from your heart.

5. Turn from them by not joining them in thought or deed.

Not long ago, I was speaking at a large church that just happened to have a Christ-centered recovery program. After I spoke, a man tapped my shoulder: "Remember me?" It took me a minute, but I eventually recognized Dave. Remember him? He was the guy I told you about earlier who disconnected from everyone who cared about him when his business started going south. Well, here he stood in front of me after ten long years. He hadn't aged a bit; in fact, looked exactly like he did ten years earlier when he sat in my office on his downward slide.

After our initial greeting, he told me his story. Since not

following through with counseling at that time, he had lost his wife, his family, and had eventually gotten addicted to crack cocaine. But even though he looked the same all these years later, he said his entire life was different and that God had completely restored him. The reason? He told me he had learned to drain his wounds and take out his trash through his church's recovery program. Dave had been through some rough years, but he was now making choices that were putting him back on track. He was finding new purpose, new relationships, and most definitely new happiness.

FORGIVENESS WILL SET YOU FREE

Recently I talked to someone who has been divorced for years. She should be on to a new and fulfilling life by now. But all she could talk about was how her ex-husband did her wrong. You could tell that she was in bondage. She just could not let it go; she was stuck in the "I can't believe he did that. He should have . . ." I often hear the same thing from adult children who have been stuck in emotional issues for decades, still blaming their parents for what they did wrong.

It is essential that you talk about what others have done to you to be healed. I am not saying to deny it. Work through the pain and get healing and understanding from people who are there for you. But at some point, *if you cannot let it go and forgive them, you are in bondage to the ones who hurt you.* As long as you hold a grudge, they still have power over your life. You are not free from what they did to you. You may think you are punishing them, but you are only punishing yourself. They don't feel your pain.

When we hang on to unforgiveness or bitterness, we drag old garbage into new relationships and situations. Just think if you moved into a new house and brought the garbage from your old one and dumped it into the living room. No one would do that, but in relationships and life we do it every day. Either old bitterness toward someone in the past gets turned onto someone in the present, or an old hurt from someone in the present is still alive in the way we deal with the person today. As a result, the energy that is tied up in still nursing our grudge is not available for a new, good life for us. The grudge has not been released, so the space is unavailable. And our view of them is tarnished.

IF YOU CANNOT LET IT GO AND FORGIVE THEM, YOU ARE IN BONDAGE TO THE ONES WHO HURT YOU.

Why would any of us want to continue to carry around all that bad stuff that someone did over a lifetime? Forgive it, and it will lose its power. Forgiveness is the only thing that will set you free.

Let it go. It is the best medicine. As the Bible says,

> Put up with each other, and forgive
> anyone who does you wrong,
> just as Christ has forgiven you.[33]

Forgiveness is one of the most important ingredients to being a happy person. If you cannot let things go, they will pollute your soul. To forgive means simply "to cancel the debt." After you forgive, the other person no longer owes you what can never be repaid anyway, so there is nothing to be mad about any more. It is finally over.

I know many people who have been horribly abused, abandoned, used, and betrayed . . . *who now have wonderful, fulfilling lives. Because . . . they have forgiven the ones who hurt them. Those abusers no longer have any power over them.* I also know many people who have suffered the same hurts and have not forgiven, and they remain stuck, even decades later, as they will not cancel the debt and let it go. They think that forgiving would mean losing power to the other person, letting them off the hook. In reality, the other person is not hurt by the grudge; only the grudge holder is hurt. Remember: a lack of forgiveness hurts the person who is not forgiving.

SUFFERING CAN BE GOOD, IF IT'S THE RIGHT KIND

All of this "facing the negative emotions" stuff can be really hard. It is not easy to face our pain, our badness, and our unforgiveness. It's no picnic. Even though it hurts to face our hurts, it also heals. So in this sense, suffering can be a good thing.

Now, by that I do not mean that suffering *itself* is good for you. Bad things happen that are not good at all. If you were abused, there is no way that was good. God feels for you in whatever has happened to make you hurt. What we are talking about here is different. It is about *facing things that are already inside you.*

The suffering that heals is not like the original pain. *It is a different kind of suffering.* If you go through something and get hurt, that is unavoidable. But if you do the right kind of suffering—the second suffering that heals—you face your pain and work through it. The event that hurt you is the first suffering. The dealing with the pain that the event caused you is the second suffering. And that is the one that heals. Then your suffering will end. This intentional suffering is the only kind of distress that ends suffering. Grief, confession, and forgiveness all hurt like the pulling of a tooth. But, like a root canal, they get the infection and pain out, and you are healthier and stronger after the procedure.

Everyone has to suffer, and some much more than others, because of the horrible things that happen. But don't add to your pain by avoiding the suffering that heals, for it can bring an end to the pain of whatever you have gone through.

A GOOD LIFE DOESN'T DEPEND ON GOOD CIRCUMSTANCES

I have learned how to be content with whatever I have.
—PHILIPPIANS 4:11 NLT

In the Bible we read amazing stories about people like the apostle Paul, who while in prison actually praised God and wrote letters to others about happiness. This is quite impressive, but if God is to be real in our lives, it helps to see evidence we can relate to today. And that is exactly what we do see. As a psychologist, I walk through some of the most difficult times of life with people, and I have seen over and over again that God meets people at the depths. And when things are hard, he gives them peace and sustenance.

It really is true that happiness is a result of what you believe and what you do, not a result of what happens to you. If you understand this, you can have a happy life.

LIFE ON THE ROCK

Most people think they will be happy if things go well or if such and such happens: "If I could just get that job, or that person, or that house, or have this relationship work out." Their well-being

Secrets about Happine

depends on what is happening to them and around them. And when good things happen, they are happy . . . for a moment. But having no inner happiness of their own, they lose their fleeting happiness as soon as something goes wrong. It is like being lost at sea with no compass, anchor, or harbor. If the water is smooth and the sun is shining, you have a nice day. But if not . . . it can get really bad.

Want to know the secret of having a good life that is not dependent on the stock market, your wacky family, your boss, or whether or not you make that sale or get that relationship you have been pining for? Here is how Jesus described this secret:

> Everyone who hears these words of mine and puts them into practice is like a wise man who built his house on the rock. The rain came down, the streams rose, and the winds blew and beat against that house; yet it did not fall, because it had its foundation on the rock. But everyone who hears these words of mine and does not put them into practice is like a foolish man who built his house on sand. The rain came down, the streams rose, and the winds blew and beat against that house, and it fell with a great crash.[34]

When we are grounded in the foundation of Christ and his words, having *put them into practice*, as he says here, then no matter what life throws at us day to day, we can rise above it and still be secure. Our happiness is based not on what happens to us but on what and *who* we believe in and what we do.

REAL-LIFE RISING ABOVE

This is no pie in the sky or denial of the things that hurt in life. Believe me, as a psychologist, I would never tell you to deny the pain of life. What I am telling you is that if you build your life on a strong relationship with God and put his secrets into practice, you can have joy and peace even when things are not as you would like them. That is living both a *real life* and a *victorious life*, to use an old-time phrase. You can be one of those people who rises above it all. Here are some of the things God will do to help you *rise above*:

- *Give you supernatural power and strength* when circumstances are beyond your own ability. You can lean on him and ask for that power moment by moment.

- *Provide you with a real sense of his presence* in times of trouble. You will feel him there with you.

- *Show you that he has a bigger purpose* for you and your life than whatever you are going through and that your life is a long book that goes way past the chapter you are in.

- *Bring good out of even the worst* things that can occur.

- *Protect you and preserve you*, even when bad things happen to you. He will keep you.

- *Fill you with his love and peace* in the midst of trouble.

- *Guide you to the answers you need* for whatever you are going through.

- *Intervene and change the situation,* sometimes supernaturally, and deliver you.

- *Grow in you new values and tastes* that are not dependent on circumstances. The things that will matter to you will be eternal, like his love and the love of your spiritual community, family, and friends.

- *Speak to you through his Word* supernaturally as well as encourage you and guide you.

- *Open new doors as old ones close* or bad events take them away. There is always a tomorrow with God.

I love Jesus's metaphor of building a house on a firm foundation, or "rock." I live in Southern California, and if you have watched CNN or other national news over the years, you have seen beautiful homes, with beautiful views, worth millions of dollars, come sliding down hills and into the mud. Worth nothing and a total loss. I always feel for those homeowners, as usually they have lost it all.

But there are other homes that do not slide down hills when storms come. They are the ones, as Jesus said, that are built on firm ground, rock-solid ground. And when the rains come, that ground does not move, and they are still there *in the midst of the storm.* Those homeowners are not asked to evacuate; they are at peace, and dry.

That is exactly how God wants us to live on the inside. Grounded, in him, in faith, in our close relationships of spiritual community, in his Word, and with his Spirit, knowing that God's love is bigger than any bad day.

BEEN THERE, DONE THAT

One of the hallmarks of mature people is that they do not have to relearn the same lesson over and over. "Been there, done that" is a phrase that you often hear wise people say as they look at some op-

GOD'S LOVE IS
BIGGER THAN
ANY BAD DAY.

tion that they refuse to choose again. They went through something similar and learned its lesson, and they do not want to repeat it.

On the other hand, immature people do not learn. They repeat. And at the heart of that repetition is the way they face difficult circumstances. They tend to see a difficulty as an unfair intrusion into the happy life they deserve, just because they exist. They get angry, blamey, and bitter when things don't go their way. They protest with a clenched fist at whomever: the boss, the market, God, or just life. But the last thing they do is ask themselves, *What can I learn from this? How can I grow through this? What growth step is this situation asking me to take? What do I need to do to make it better?* If they could do this, their bad circumstance would not be a total loss. Then the next time they came across that kind of person or situation, they would either not get involved, or they would negotiate it differently and better. They might even fix the situation itself.

God gives us a great perspective and wisdom on how to navigate a hard time:

> *Consider it a sheer gift, friends,*
> *when tests and challenges come at you from all sides.*
> *You know that under pressure, your faith-life*
> *is forced into the open and shows its true colors.*
> *So don't try to get out of anything prematurely.*
> *Let it do its work so you become mature and well-developed,*
> *not deficient in any way.*
> *If you don't know what you're doing, pray to the Father.*
> *He loves to help. You'll get his help,*
> *and won't be condescended to when you ask for it.*[35]

So there we are: don't protest the unfairness of life. Who said life was meant to be fair, anyway? Trials and pressures come. Protesting them is a little like yelling at gravity because we don't like it. They are a part of life. But when challenges do come, work through them with faith—or as the verse above says, allow it to "do its work so you become mature and well-developed." Ask God for wisdom, knowing that "he loves to help."

Couples who do handle hardship this way, for example, do

not divorce quickly and then repeat their mistakes in another relationship. They persevere and learn the lesson of their trials. Then, they are more complete and able to have an even better relationship together after God has taught them what they need to know. But if one of them is not willing to hang in there, and the marriage ends, at least the one who learned through the process will ultimately go on to make a better choice the next time, instead of repeating the pattern.

The same thing is true in business. In fact, good leaders even put their protégés into situations that challenge them past their abilities in order to "try" them and "grow" them. As a result of those hard times, their people become more complete and able to lead something bigger. The ones who don't learn how to deal with the challenges? They usually get an "opportunity to be successful in another company"—i.e., fired—where they will repeat their mistakes with another boss they can blame. And their first leader is usually glad to donate them to a competitor.

This secret to happiness says that even when things are not going well, there are valuable lessons to be learned. But you have to look for them. So ask yourself, *What does God want to teach me in this trial? How can I use this to become a better person instead of allowing it to make me bitter? What work needs to be done in me through this difficulty?* That is the language that we hear from people we describe as "happy." Even in a hard time.

You were not meant to be alone. And yet sometimes our behavior or attitudes push away the right kind of people or attract the wrong kind. We get stuck in relationship patterns and think we can't get out. But we can. When you activate God's secrets in your life, you will discover newfound confidence, deeper relationships, and the kind of fulfillment you long for.

God has some secrets about how to attract and be attractive to the right kind of people. In the following pages you'll learn some secrets about how to do that and make relationships work.

Secrets about Relationships

GOOD RELATIONSHIPS COME FROM HAVING THE SKILLS TO PRODUCE THEM

Do to others as you would like them to do to you.

—LUKE 6:31 NLT

A pastor was counseling a couple and gave them the following feedback: "The problem with you guys is that you want a 'ten' relationship, but you are both 'fives.'"

Oooooh. What a stinger. But as a psychologist, I love it. I understood exactly what he was telling them. They would never have the kind of relationship they wanted until they possessed the relationship skills to produce it. It just can't happen. You can't win the Super Bowl if you can't block, tackle, and pass.

It reminds me of a couple I was working with. The woman, in her early thirties, wanted to leave her husband because of a conflict they had been having for a while. Certainly he had some issues that caused her pain, which he was working on and changing. Of course he wasn't perfect, so some of her complaints were valid.

But she was completely unaware of how her own attitudes and behaviors were contributing to the problems. She was sarcastic and biting in her comments about him. She would not acknowledge any improvement he made and basically saw him as "all bad." At the same time, she had the fantasy that if she just got a divorce and started over with someone else, it would be "all good." She thought she had "made a mistake" in marrying him and that if she just found the "right person," all would be wonderful. She was sure a new relationship would be awesome.

Finally I just had to tell her: "The only problem with a new relationship is that *you* would be a part of it. There is no way it could be awesome, no matter what perfect guy was in it."

She looked at me with a stunned, frozen look. "What?"

"You think that a good relationship would come from 'finding someone new.' And I am telling you that you do not possess the skills to have a good relationship, no matter who you might find. That is why I think you had better stay right where you are and learn how to have a relationship with the man you're married to. Until you do, you will be incapable of a positive relationship with *anyone*."

Needless to say, we had a lot to talk about after that. I told her that if she ever considered leaving, it should be for the reasons that God defines. And those are always where someone is an innocent party to a betrayal. She had better first get her own relational act together and do everything right before she defined her misery as "all his fault." Those scenarios do exist, but this was not one of them.

We can only have relationships that equal our own ability. So if we want the great things that relationships offer—like love, security, and growth—then we have to be people capable of building love, providing security, and fostering growth. When we are, we can have the relationships we want. Until we are, great relationships will elude us.

> WE CAN ONLY HAVE RELATIONSHIPS THAT EQUAL OUR OWN ABILITY.

This is the big problem in the dating world. I see people over and over looking for "the one." All their energy is focused on the person they are looking for, not the person they are becoming. And as we shall see in the next secret, the two are related. But even if they found "the one," they would never be able to make it work without the necessary skills. Still, many hold on to the fantasy of instant Hollywood love. Do you believe in that? If you do, I have an assignment for you.

Go to the supermarket and look at the magazine rack. Look at the covers, and you will see several that display photos of the newest

Hollywood match-up, with headlines that shout, "So-and-So Finds True Love!" The articles will gush with enthusiasm about how the two have "found their soul mates in the other." Great. May the fantasy live on . . . until you complete your assignment. Go back to the supermarket six to eight months later and look for the same magazines, and you will see the truth of this secret. The cover stories will say: "The Split! What Really Happened . . . Friends Tell All."

The "soul mates" did not make it. The reason is always the same: relationships fail when the skills to make them work are not present in one or both of the people involved. There is no such thing as instant and *lasting* Hollywood love. Lasting love comes from having the skills and ability to create and maintain love. If a couple finds those abilities, then they can make it work. But until they do, the magazine stories will always be about the most recent split and the next soul mate. And the headlines will repeat themselves with a different lover.

So the secret here is this: when people have the skills to produce lasting love, they will find it.

THE GOLDEN RULE

You've probably heard of the golden rule. Maybe it's called golden because it's the kind of rule that, if you follow it, can truly change your life. Jesus is the one who taught it, and this is what it says:

Treat others the same way you want them to treat you.[1]

Sounds simple, but this maxim can revolutionalize marriages, friendships, work relationships, and family relationships. Any kind of bad relationship will be drastically affected when this rule is followed day in and day out.

There are two people in any relationship, and the only one *you* have control over is you. So if you want to have good relationships, do not just look for the "right people" (although as we will see later, that is certainly important), but work on having the skills that produce the kind of relationship you want. And that starts by treating the other person the way you want to be treated.

> LOVE, KINDNESS, FORGIVENESS, FAITHFULNESS, HONESTY, ACCEPTANCE, AUTHENTICITY . . . THESE ARE WHAT PRODUCE GOOD RELATIONSHIPS.

There are things you must bring to the table if you expect to have good relationships. You have to be the first one to bring the important skills of love, kindness, forgiveness, faithfulness, honesty, acceptance, authenticity, and other such important traits. If you don't, you will be a "five" wanting a "ten" relationship. Or you will find a ten and then bring the other person down. There will be no love if you do not bring love to the table yourself.

GIVE BETTER THAN YOU GET

One of my favorite verses in the Bible gives a formula for making a bad relationship better and keeping a good one good:

Do not be overcome by evil,
but overcome evil with good.[2]

Give *better* than you get. Imagine if both people in a relationship lived by this rule. Think of it this way: when two people fall in love and get married, or when two people become friends, they do it for good reasons. No one ever said, "I love you because you are such a jerk. Marry me!" (Unless, of course, they are sicker than this book can deal with.) Most relationships form because people are good to each other and are mutually satisfied. Until . . .

One of them has a bad day and says something sarcastic. The other one gets hurt and says something less than loving back. Then the first one withdraws, etc. In other words, the relationship is good until one of them gives something that is less than good. Then the other one returns less than good, and they are on a downward slide.

Now, we all do that. But the person who knows how to give better than he gets will quickly turn the situation around by swallowing his pride or seeing what a snit he is being, and going to the other and saying, "I'm sorry. I am just being a brat. Forgive me." Then the relationship turns back upward, and the downward slide is stopped. We see how this verse works when we overcome dysfunction with health, when we do not give dysfunction for dysfunction—when we give better than we get.

In other relationships, however, one person pulls the other one down into his or her worst self. One person's dysfunction brings out the dysfunction in the other, and all it takes to go down the wrong road is one failure. No one can get above it, and it all goes downhill.

Giving better than you get also means that when someone fails you, you give him or her what *you* yourself need when you are not giving your best: you need help. Sometimes you need understanding and kindness, acceptance of where you are. Sometimes you may need a kind piece of honesty, a confrontation. But whatever it is you need, you need something *good, not bad. You need something redemptive when you are at your worst, not something hurtful. You need help.* You need an "Oh . . . sorry things are bad," instead of "Watch your lip."

Give good for evil, and you will find that the fights are harder to have. Or at least, to last. Be redemptive, and serve the other person. Extend yourself like God did for us when he came to our level and suffered innocently for us, trying to bring us up to his level. Your significant other needs that from you, and you need to do that in order to have the relationship get better. Give back better than you get if you want your relationship to thrive.

BEFORE YOU SPEAK . . .

So before you speak, make sure that your speech is filled with the skills of love—practicing the golden rule and giving back better than you get. Remember, whatever you say is either building love or tearing it down. As Proverbs tells us,

> *The tongue has the power of life and death,*
> *and those who love it will eat its fruit.*[3]

You will eat the fruit of what you say and do in your relationships, day after day and year after year. Build the skills to say the things that produce love, and you will find love.

YOU ATTRACT TO YOURSELF RELATIONSHIPS THAT FIT YOU

Trouble chases sinners,
while blessings reward the righteous.

—PROVERBS 13:21 NLT

"I don't understand it. I can be in a coliseum of fifty thousand people, and I am going to somehow fall in love with the only alcoholic in the crowd. It is uncanny. I just draw them in like moths to a light."

"If there is a control freak in the entire state, I will find him and think I can't live without him."

"I keep going to work for jerks. It seems that if I get offered a job by a jerk, I automatically think it is the best company in the world . . . until I have been there for six months."

"I keep finding losers. What is it about me that attracts these guys?"

"Why do all of the women I am attracted to turn out to be so needy?"

"I keep finding myself in the same relationship over and over; the only thing that changes is the names."

You know what I love about these statements? Whenever I hear them, whether it is about dating, friendship, business, or choosing a community, I know the people who make them are on the road to finding better relationships. Why? Because they are finally noticing that the *people* they are finding are not the problem after all. Instead, they are seeing that *they* are the problem, or at least a big part of it: They are realizing that the real problem is that their own "people picker" is broken.

They keep choosing the ones who are either going to hurt them or let them down or not be good for them in some way. And they are beginning to realize that it is no accident that these people show up in their lives: they themselves have something to do with finding—and attracting—them. When I hear that insight, I know it's only a matter of time until the pattern ends. Once they notice it, they can get to the reasons for it and change them. And you can too.

Like Attracts Like

But it is so, so hard to *get* people to realize that they have a part in attracting these people into their lives, and for being attracted to them too. They often do not see that what is so attractive to them about the person in the beginning has something to do with their own dysfunction and that they deny obvious warning signs. I wish I had a dollar for every time I've heard, "I saw little signs that, looking back, I ignored. I guess I just wanted it to be right so much that I ignored some things that really were red flags." They did not listen to "that little voice inside."

There is a law of attraction in this area of life for sure. Dysfunctional people attract dysfunctional people, and healthy people attract healthy people. It's uncanny how consistent it is. There is just no such thing, for example, as someone who is in a long-term relationship with an addict who is not in some way codependent. Those two are always able to find each other. The question is, *why?*

The Secret would say that it is the law of attraction working in the sphere of energy. The energies of each person literally draw them to each other. I have no scientific way of knowing whether or not that is true. But we certainly see the reality of the attraction itself. I do believe that we have energy fields that are part of our character, and there

THE REAL PROBLEM IS THAT THEIR "PEOPLE PICKER" IS BROKEN.

probably is something to that. For example, you can just feel it when someone is full of love and also when someone has a "dark" energy to them as well. Some people can just walk into a room and either light it up or turn out the lights. You can feel the whole mood change. Maybe someday there will be a meter to measure people's energy or light and dark levels.

But I can explain it in more natural ways than energy alone. *There are character dynamics that explain attraction and how we are drawn to certain kinds of people and not to others.* Let's take codependents, for example. It is part of their makeup to need someone to fix, to repair, to make better. They are rescuers. Now think about this. What do rescuers need?

Exactly. A person to rescue. And what kind of people needs rescuing? Responsible people? No. Responsible people take care of themselves. The kind who need rescuing are those who are not taking responsibility and ownership of their own lives and are a mess. So codependent people will always have irresponsible people or addicts in their lives until they realize that their codependency is what makes those relationships exist and necessitates their having problem people in their lives.

Likewise, on the other side of the equation, if people are *not* taking responsibility for themselves, what kind of people do they need? Rescuers. Someone to take care of them. Voilà! There's your match. They find each other. In some sort of unconscious way, they have the ability to sense each other, and the match is made, even across a crowded room. They hear fireworks when they meet. They just like each other. It feels right or familiar. They have no idea what is driving that attraction, but they just know that it feels good in the beginning. It's after the dynamics begin to kick in that it all unfolds.

Let's take another example. If someone is really controlling and does not respect another person's boundaries, what kind of person is he or she going to be looking for? What kind of person "fits" with a controller? Answer: *Someone who will allow that behavior.* It's a perfect match. It all feels so natural. So they are drawn to each other like magnets:

- the selfish one and the selfless one
- the perfectionist and the guilty people-pleaser
- the detached one and the one who is afraid of real intimacy
- the emotionally unavailable person and the one who has been abandoned all her life
- the one with the negative self-image and the critical one
- the self-centered one and the giver
- the narcissistic one and the flatterer
- the overly "good girl" and the "bad boy"

I heard someone say once that you are attracted to people at your same level of sickness or health. That is definitely not true. I have seen pretty healthy people with a few issues pair up with really sick—and even evil—people. They were not "equally" messed up. But here is what was true: *their issues were compatible in a sick sort of way.* An abuser is often sicker than the passive person he abuses. You can see how their dynamics fit well together, nevertheless. They may not be equal, but they are compatible. It works, if you will.

IT'S ABOUT YOU

So here is the way to unlock this secret: take responsibility for the fact that if you are drawn to dysfunctional people in friendship, romance, business, or spiritual community . . . there is a reason.

It is about you, not them. Find out why you are attracted to them. Here is an example: I have a friend who is single and for a couple of years has been griping to me about the guys she dates. She whines and complains about how noncommittal they are and how they don't follow through or take initiative in the relationship. She always feels they don't plan or do normal responsible things required in a relationship. Finally, I was tired of the same story and her saying, "What is it with guys nowadays? There are no good ones." So I told her what I thought.

"I think that you are getting what you are attracted to, which is little boys," I said.

"What are you talking about?" she said.

"Just that. I think that all these guys are little boys. Everyone of them is in his late twenties or early thirties and somehow still tied in to 'Daddy.' One of them worked for his dad, not able to make it on his own. Another lived at home with his father. Another worked in the same company as his father, where his father got him the job; and another one had financial ties. All of them, still not on their own, and they dated like it. They just wanted someone else to please *them* and didn't want to do anything that smacked of an adult relationship."

I explained this over and over, but she would not agree. To her, it was all about there being no good ones "out there." Then it happened.

"Oh my," she said. "I had a moment of enlightenment."

"What happened? One of your little boys get a job?" I asked.

"No. I had a date with what I think you would call a 'man.' He is a portfolio manager, put himself through law school, and takes lots of classes on leadership, personal growth, and all that stuff. It was so different," she said.

"That's awesome," I said. "So, what happened?"

"I was sitting there listening to him at dinner and just finding out about his life when I found myself wanting to leave and end the date. So I tuned in to what was going on with me and realized . . . I felt about one inch tall around him. Being around a real adult, I realized, threatened me. I need to be in control, and with this guy, I felt really out of control—even though he was exactly the kind of guy I have been griping that the others were not! *I am totally afraid of what I say I want.* I can see what you are talking about. I choose little boys so I won't be threatened," she said, amazed and convicted. Caught.

At last I felt hope for her.

PLAY YOUR OWN GAME

I once told a woman who asked, "How do you deal with critical people?" to just be honest with them. "If you will, you will never hear from them again." The tip is this: stop playing their game. Stop playing the game that works with their dysfunction, and you will stop attracting them. And the people who are already playing the "unhealthy" game with you will get the picture and begin to play your game—the healthy one. Honesty, responsibility, love, faithfulness, commitment. Let that be your game, and the only kind of people who will come knocking will be people of like character. The others want no part of it.

*M*ISPLACED TRUST OPENS THE DOOR TO MISERY

A righteous man is cautious in friendship,
but the way of the wicked leads them astray.

—PROVERBS 12:26 NIV

From the moment you are born, until the day you die, you draw life from the outside world. From God and from people. So the question becomes: what are you taking in? Trust good people, open your heart to them, and you will thrive. Trust the wrong kind of people, and you will suffer.

In the beginning of this book, we looked at trust as the key to all the other secrets—and so it is. Trust opens the door to love. Trust, we said, is the door to larger lives. Trust opens the door to God and others so that our hearts, minds, souls, and strength can take in what they have for us. When we eat food, we grow. When we take in good things from others, we grow as well. But there is another side of trust. Just as we get good things when we open ourselves up to them, so we will get ourselves in trouble when we trust in the wrong things. In the same way that it's possible to get food poisoning from rancid food, it's also possible to get heart, mind, soul, and strength poisoning from toxic people.

Here is the simple truth of how God created life to work: we get it from others. We take it in. When you take in good, good will multiply in you. You will live a life greater than your wildest dreams as you soar on the "wind beneath your wings" that they provide. You will gain wisdom, love, strength, support, healing, growth, skills, maturity of your talents, understanding, knowledge, joy, and on and on. The Bible says that God hands out his

TRUST IS JUST A DOOR. IT IS NOT MAGIC.

"goodies," his "grace," through the good people in our lives, using their gifts to help us grow.[4] You know this from your own life. Think of the good people who have helped you in the ways that you are thriving.

But trust is just a door. It is not magic. It always has an object on the other end. What and who you put your trust in is what matters. Just as trust can be the door to good things, it can be the door to great misery as well. So this secret is one of the most powerful taught in all the Bible: Be careful whom you trust. Misplaced trust can open the door to great misery.

TWO SOURCES OF PAIN

There are many kinds of pain, but two that I want to focus on here. The first is the kind that happens to innocent people at the hand of evil or bad people who abuse them, injure them, use them, betray them, or do something horrible that the sufferer had no part in whatsoever. Either in childhood or adulthood, a very bad person causes the victim horrible suffering. It is awful, and it is one of the things that God screams about. *He hates it when the innocent suffer:*

> *This is God's Message: Attend to matters of justice.*
> *Set things right between people.*
> *Rescue victims from their exploiters.*
> *Don't take advantage of the homeless,*
> *the orphans, the widows.*
> *Stop the murdering!*[5]

It is a terrible thing to see the innocent suffer, and God is always deeply moved when it happens. He asks us to be his arms and hands to relieve the suffering of others. When we do, he says, "Whatever you did for one of the least of these . . . , you did for me."[6]

The second kind of pain is the kind that comes at the hands of bad, evil, or at least irresponsible and self-centered people. But it is not like the first, where the victim is a child or is somehow overpowered. It is not an unavoidable kind of suffering. *It is the kind that comes from trusting the wrong kind of person.*

We, and I say "we" because we have all had this happen at some time or another, should have seen it coming, and yet for some reason, we trusted the wrong people. Sometimes we were unaware of what was happening, and other times we had plenty of warning and should have seen it coming. As we all know, it's not always possible to see it coming. For people change, and in different contexts they may become untrustworthy. But often it can be seen and avoided if we are careful. The point here is that *this second kind of suffering comes as a result of misplaced trust.*

Now that does not mean that we should not empathize with people who bring crises on their own heads or that we do not care and help people when they get themselves into messes. But the message for us is that *the problem could have been avoided, and the lesson is this: learn from it, and avoid it next time!*

You know people who have been hurt by trusting the wrong kind of person. Maybe you are one of those people. The signs were there, and they were ignored. But the wish for something more, better, or different was stronger than the screaming reality.

I have seen people believe the unbelievable and go forward with a relationship or a business deal when the signs or the track record was just so clearly speaking to them and telling them to stop!

So ask yourself a question: what do you trust?

Do you trust what people tell you? Do you trust their charm? Do you trust their personalities? Do you trust how much you are attracted to them? Do you trust their credentials? Their power or status?

What is it that makes you open yourself up to someone and give them access to your:

- heart
- mind
- soul
- strength

- time
- family
- friends
- talents

- information
- possessions
- dreams
- plans

- passion
- money
- desires
- love
- hopes
- faith

How you answer that question is one of the most revealing things about you. We live in a culture where people give themselves quickly to people in love, sex, and romance all the time. They get a match online and go on a vacation together without even knowing if the other person has a parole officer! People enter into business relationships without doing their "due diligence." People become instant intimate friends without really knowing the other person and yet trust them with their deepest secrets.

Here is a secret that the Bible and any good psychologist would tell you about trust: trust a person's character, as evidenced by their behavior.[7]

CHEAP TALK

The street version of this is "talk is cheap." People will tell you anything, but doing it is another matter. Do not believe what people *say*. Believe what they *do*. What they actually do is what you are going to have to live with and what you can depend on, which is the essence of trust. We can depend only on what people do, not what they say they will do or what we wish they would do.

So the secret is to watch people's behavior. Watch their performance. Do not listen to excuses, but observe them over time. Time is a key ingredient to trust. Here is the way Jesus put it:

> *A good tree produces good fruit, and a*
> *bad tree produces bad fruit. . . .*
> *Just as you can identify a tree by its fruit,*
> *so you can identify people by their actions.*[8]

In dating, trust someone who does more than look good, is charming, or tells you things that sound good. Trust the person who treats you with love and respect over time, showing that he or she has the ability to put you and the relationship as a priority over his or her own selfish needs. Trust someone who shows that she values love, freedom, responsibility, God, kindness, commitment, and things that last.

In marriage, when someone has made a serious mistake, like a betrayal or an addiction, trust him not when he *says* he's sorry and just promises to do better. That is a great beginning, but that is just a beginning. Trust him when his "sorry" has become a path you can see: when he is getting treatment and staying with it, when he is involved in recovery, or has changed the people he hangs around with, or develops accountability relationships, or is seeking help, etc. Trust the path you can see.

In business, trust someone who has a track record of performance, happy ex-partners, a path of success, a clean record, and good clean financials. And make sure you have enough time to check all of that out.

In friendship, trust someone you have known long enough to see that they are honest, loyal, spiritual, responsible, kind, forgiving, trustworthy, and possess other qualities that ensure good treatment.

Sometimes in a seminar I read the following psalm of David that tells who he is willing to trust and who he is not. Then I ask the audience a question: "If you had practiced what David says here since you were age eighteen, would you have avoided some pain?" Read what he says:

> I will refuse to look at anything vile and vulgar.
> I hate all who deal crookedly;
> I will have nothing to do with them.
> I will reject perverse ideas
> and stay away from every evil.
> I will not tolerate people who slander their neighbors.
> I will not endure conceit and pride.
> I will search for faithful people to be my companions.
> Only those who are above reproach
> will be allowed to serve me.
> I will not allow deceivers to serve in my house,
> and liars will not stay in my presence.[9]

Just to make it relevant to your life, *vile* means "destructive" and *perverse* means "distorted" or "crooked."

He's telling us to avoid and have nothing to do with people who are not faithful, those who have destructive behavior, who talk about people falsely, are arrogant and look down on you, who are proud and who deceive you or lie to you. Now, let me ask you: would your life since age eighteen have been any different if you had lived by that? You get it.

THE NEW GUY

Recently I was on an airplane and overheard two flight attendants talking. One of them had a "new guy," as she put it.

"I can't wait to get there. I'm going to drive out and spend the weekend with my new guy. He is sooo great," she said.

"Fun. That sounds wonderful," her friend said.

"Yes . . . he is such a good guy," she said. "It is so good."

This is where you should not have a psychologist standing next to the galley waiting to get into the bathroom. "So, how long have you known him?" I asked.

"A month," she said. "He is a really good one."

"And you really think you can know that in a month?" I quizzed her.

"What do you mean?" she asked, with a look of "What is he talking about?" on her face.

"Well, just remember . . . there are sprinters and there are marathon men," I said.

"What is that?" she asked.

"Anyone can look good for a month," I said. "Judging from your level of excitement, I think you need to take her along as a chaperone," I added, pointing to her friend. "The sprinters are the ones who look really good in the beginning but can't run the whole race. The marathon men are the ones who don't just start well, but finish well. That takes time to determine. Just be careful," I said.

"You are not kidding," she said. "That is true. I have been married three times, so I know that!" I hope she does. It sounds like she has had other times when she thought a guy was "great" and it did not turn out that way.

"I hope your friend doesn't let you take the minister along for the weekend. Don't need another wedding so soon," I said. We had a good laugh, but I think she got the point.

GET YOUR SENSES BACK

Figure out why you tend to trust people when they are not trustworthy. You may be too needy, and that blinds you to who they really are. You may have such idealized wishes that you can't see reality. You see what you want to see, not what is. But the Bible's advice is, *get your senses back.*

> *Solid food is for the mature,*
> *who because of practice have their senses trained*
> *to discern good and evil.*[10]

Use your past experience, your "practice," to train you. Do not make the same mistake again. Listen to your "senses." Be careful who you trust—with your heart, your dreams, your soul. This is how Jesus put it:

Do not give what is holy to dogs,
and do not throw your pearls before swine.[11]

That is a good secret to know. Listen to that little voice inside, and do not go forward when there are warning signs. "Trust God, and lock your car"—no matter how safe the parking lot looks.

LISTEN AND VALIDATE BEFORE ALL ELSE

My dear brothers, take note of this:
Everyone should be quick to listen,
slow to speak and slow to become angry.

—JAMES 1:19 NIV

The couple I was talking to was the kind that everyone looks at and says, "They are such nice people . . . how could they be having problems?" And that was true. Both of them were very nice, at least to everyone else. She was a public relations executive, whom everyone loved; and he was an HR director, who often helped other people. But with each other they had found a way to disconnect, to be very unloving, and were acting anything but nice. Very little felt nice about her cold indifference and sarcasm toward him or his negative reactions to her expressions of displeasure.

"I just don't feel cared about or taken care of by him. Bottom line is that I don't feel loved," she began. "I feel really alone. He doesn't do anything to prove that he loves me or cares."

"That's not true," he said quickly. "I do a lot of things that show how much I love her. I do a ton of stuff for her. The other day I . . ." He went on to list several things that he had done that, to him, proved how caring he was.

"Yeah, but that is not what I needed," she said. "What he doesn't get is that . . ." She began a list of how the things he did were not loving.

From there, he jumped back in and explained why she was not getting it and how much he was doing for her, when I jumped in. "Let me ask you something," I said to him. "What are you hoping she will get from what you're saying? Are you trying to get her to see that she is wrong and you are right? That you have been doing a lot of loving things and she is just not getting it? Is that what you are looking for, to be *right*?"

"Well . . . not really . . . I mean . . . sort of. I want her to see that I *am* doing things for her. What she is saying about me not loving her is not true. I want her to see it," he said.

"Well, if you were in court, then I guess proving your side to a judge or jury would be worth something," I said. "You would be right, shown to be not guilty of being the bad husband, and win the case. And she would lose. But then where would you be with her?

"What you are missing is that no matter how 'right' you are about doing things that *you* feel are loving, the reality is this: *she is not feeling loved by you.*

"Are you hearing that? I don't care how right you are right now. I just want to know if you are hearing that?" I asked.

"Now that you say it like that, I do," he said. "So what do I do?"

That question is what this secret is about.

"Why don't you try listening and validating what she tells you regarding *her* experience?" I asked.

"Like how? What do you mean?" he asked. At that moment, I understood their years of pain. They probably had never done that.

"What if, instead of trying to convince her that you are right and she is wrong about what she is feeling, you just listened and tried to understand her experience and showed her that you get it. This wouldn't mean that your reality is not also true, at least for you. But it would show her that her reality means something to you and that you are willing to see and understand what she is trying to tell you. What if, instead of trying to show her why she is wrong, you said this:

"'So you feel totally uncared for and not taken care of . . . oh . . . That's terrible to feel that uncared for. That would be awful . . . I would never want you to feel like that, and it is the last thing I want you to feel. But I get it. You do feel that way. No matter what I think I am doing to show you, it is not helping you to feel loved. I hear you.'"

At that moment she began to cry. It was the first time I had seen any softness from her in the process. The rest of the time she had been very hard, and when she did talk, her words had a somewhat haughty, sarcastic edge to them. Her tears, though, were true vulnerability, without which a marriage cannot thrive, and until she was listened to, that vulnerability had no place to go.

FINDING THE OTHER PERSON'S HEART IS MORE IMPORTANT THAN GETTING THAT PERSON TO SEE THAT YOU ARE RIGHT.

From there, we had a really helpful discussion as he began to see something: *finding the other person's heart is more important than getting that person to see that you are right*.

It did not matter if he thought he was being loving. She did not feel loved. If he could hear that, he then could use that same effort and care to do something that would make her feel loved. But until he could listen and not try to convince, that was not going to happen.

WHEN SOMEONE FINALLY HEARS

Have you ever had this experience? You called tech support and told them of your problem, and the tech guy said, "Do such and such." So, you did it, and it still didn't work. You tell him, and he says, "Well it should work now. We do that all the time, and it works. So it should be okay." But it is still not working! You want to climb through the phone line at that point, right? I find myself saying, "I know you think it should be working. But can you hear me telling you that it is *not* working? I know it should, but it is not. What it should be doing is not helping me. Can you help me or not?" At that point I hope they don't have caller ID and figure out that I am a psychologist who writes books on how to communicate and have good relationships, because we are doing neither. And it goes nowhere. Until . . .

You call back and get a different person. This time you tell the tech guy your problem and he says, "Oh no! That's so frustrating. That should not happen to you . . . let me see how I can help and get it fixed for you." I want to scream, "Thank you, Jesus! You sent me an angel!" It just feels so good for someone to finally hear.

THE FEAR

Many people are afraid to validate how another person feels because they fear that it means they agree with the other person. And since sometimes the other person is just wrong, they don't want to do that. But here is the point: it does not matter if they are wrong, because you are not "giving up" your position if you validate theirs. When the husband understands how the wife feels and validates that *it is true that she feels that way,* he is in no way agreeing that he is a bad husband who is not trying to love her. All he is doing is validating that, no matter what he is doing, it is still true that she does not feel loved.

He has not lost himself if he does that. When you empathize with a teenager who is screaming, "It's not fair! You're a mean parent!" you do not believe that what your child is saying is true. But if you do not learn to hear that she feels that way and connect with that feeling, you may lose your connection to her heart. All it takes is "I am so sorry it feels that way. That's terrible. Tell me what feels mean."

Then you can hear it and empathize *and* still keep your limit. You can hear something, listen to how it is for the other person, and still say no. But at least the person feels understood and cared for in the process. People can accept no and be okay as long as they are heard and understood. What we cannot accept is not being heard or listened to or cared for in the process.

THE BEGINNING

This secret begins with the stance that St. Francis of Assisi suggested in his famous prayer:

O Divine Master,
grant that I may not so much seek to be consoled as to console;
to be understood, as to understand.

The beginning focus is not just to "get our point across," but to make sure that the other people get a chance to get theirs across as well. Then you have connected to the heart. Once you do that, problems can be solved.

And after you take the beginning stance of seeking to understand, the next step is to make sure that they know you understand. Remember this rule: You have not understood someone

a stand and the relationship gets sick, or anger turns against you and attacks you instead. This is what happens when people who, rather than standing up for themselves, attack themselves instead of the problem. "I'm so stupid; I hate myself" usually means they have been hurt by someone they cannot stand up to and have turned the anger against themselves. Another unhealthy way we use anger is to react with a ballistic display when a little bit would have done the job. We should not get enraged when a little discussion about the problem would suffice.

So the secret to anger is just like the verse says: "Be angry, and yet do not sin; do not let the sun go down on your anger." You have to "be angry." If you are going to protect and preserve the good things, you need to feel your anger to know that something is wrong. *It is your signal.* But when you do, do not sin in the way you use it. Here are the tips:

1. *Be angry . . . and feel it.* This means that you need to be aware of your feelings so you know when something is wrong.

2. *Use anger for something "good."* Ask yourself if what you're angry about is worth protecting. Sometimes we use anger to protect bad things, like pride or our own control. Make sure that your anger is just and righteous, meaning that there really is a threat to something worth protecting. Our pride is not worth protecting, but our love is.

3. *Use self-control*—don't do anything rash. Bring your head
to the problem as well as your feelings. Take a time-out,
and think about what the real problem is and how you are
going to address it. If necessary, talk it out with someone
else. Don't make a move while you are too heated up.

4. *Use it to solve the problem.* If your anger is good and
righteous, then use it to solve the problem, not hurt the
person. "Do not sin" means that when you use your anger,
you do not hurt anyone in the process. Be kind. Take a
stand *against* the issue, but *for* the person: "I love you, but
I don't like what you did." That is a proper use of your
immune response of anger. It attacks the bacteria, not the
body. You address the problem, not the person's heart.

Those are the steps to being "good and mad." When you are
"good" in your anger, you use it to make sure good things happen,
not to hurt someone. That is how God made your anger—like a
good, relational immune system. Remember, if you don't listen
to your anger and let it do its work, you and your relationships
are going to get sicker and sicker as the infection of a problem
unaddressed only grows.

RELATIONSHIP SUCCESS EQUALS ABILITY TO CONFRONT

The Bible is clear, and the research backs it up: people who have
successful relationships use their anger well and confront prob-

lems directly. They take step four above and get active in confronting the issue directly and quickly. But there are two aspects of confrontation that successful people perform. First, they are *proactive*. Second, they are *redemptive*.

Before proactive means they do not wait to confront an issue. They do not wait, either, for the other side to come to them. Nor do they wait for the problem to get so large and poisonous that the problem itself confronts them, instead of them confronting the problem. That is a little like waiting until an abscessed tooth wakes you up in the middle of your vacation, confronting you to do something about it. It would have been much better to have gone to the dentist early on and have it taken care of.

THAT IS HOW GOD MADE YOUR ANGER—LIKE A GOOD, RELATIONAL IMMUNE SYSTEM.

So don't wait for the other side to come to you, and don't wait for the problem to get bigger. If it is a real, ongoing problem, it is like an infection, and it will *not* get better on its own. I have heard so many people say, "Well, she is the one who has the problem with me, so she needs to come to me. I am not going to call her. It is her responsibility to come to me." Not so fast, avoidant-breath. Listen to Jesus's instruction, rendered in *The Message*:

> *This is how I want you to conduct yourself in these matters.*
> *If you enter your place of worship and, about to make an offering,*
> *you suddenly remember a grudge a friend has against you,*

131

abandon your offering, leave immediately,
go to this friend and make things right.
Then and only then, come back and work things out with God.[12]

His message is clear. Be proactive, and do everything possible from your side, even if the person has not come to you. God wants you to have all your relationships and problems cleared up, as much as it depends on you. Certainly you cannot control whether or not the other side will respond well, and hopefully they will. But you can control your side of things and do all that you can do. Get proactive. Make that call. Do not wait for the problem to get worse.

And get this: Jesus says also that if we are on the other end of a conflict when we have something against someone else, we have to be proactive with that person as well. We have to go to him, not wait for him to just wake up and get it:

If a fellow believer hurts you, go and tell him—
work it out between the two of you.
If he listens, you've made a friend.[13]

So if you are going to be successful in relationships and life, you can't wait for the problem to come to you. You have to go to the problem.

The same applies not only to relationships but also to business and personal problems. Do not wait to make that call to solve a problem. Make the hard calls first, and you will be like the successful people of the world. They deal with things; they don't avoid them. Many people's credit, for example, would be saved if they would just pick up the phone, call the creditor, and work out a solution. Instead, they wait and the collection agency begins to show up like an abscessed tooth.

The second aspect of successful confrontation is being *redemptive*. What that means is that you confront a problem in a way that has the greatest possibility for a good ending. Good endings are when the problem is solved and the relationship is restored. Instead of going in and nuking the person, you preserve the person and face the objective problem.

Here are some tips:

- *Get the anger out of the way before the conversation.* Remember, your anger is the signal that something is wrong. It is the red blinking light on your dashboard. It is not a tool to fix the problem. The anger lets you know that something is wrong, and then it's job is done. It is not a communication skill, so leave the volume, the screaming, and the rage somewhere else before you go and deal with the person. God puts it this way: "A fool gives full vent to his anger, but a wise man keeps himself under control."[14] Take kindness and firmness as your tools.

- *Affirm the person and the relationship first:* "I want to talk to you about something, because I love you and our relationship is important to me." Or give an affirming comment about them first before bringing up the issue.

- *Say what you want the result to be before you begin*: "I want to talk about this so we can be closer," or "I want to talk about this so our relationship can work even better."

- *Be specific about the problem and its effects.* Use the old "when you do *a*, I feel *b*, or *b* happens": "I want you to be careful about time, because when you are late, it affects the rest of my schedule and that gets really difficult for me later in the day with other meetings."

- *Get an agreement that you are understanding the same things*: "So, what are you hearing me say?"

- *If needed, clarify*: "No, I am not saying that you are a bad assistant. I am saying that I need you to change this one thing."

- *If necessary, plan a follow-up*: "Let's talk in about a week, and see how it is going," or "What should we do if this happens again?"

- *Leave on an affirming note* of the person and the relationship.

Remember, your success in relationships and in life will be equal to your ability to confront. This makes total sense when you think about it. For success to happen, the obstacles that are standing in the way of that success must be removed. When there is an obstacle to intimacy or a goal, the intimacy or goal will not be reached until the obstacle is faced and removed. If done in a good way, the success will come.

So don't avoid anger or confrontation if you want God's success in your relationships. Let your anger tell you what is wrong, then confront with kindness and clarity. Then you will find the relationship result you desire. That is how both "good" and "mad" can help you succeed.

All of us want to feel like we are accomplishing things that matter and to be successful in what we do. But many times we either don't know what we should be doing, how to do it, or how to make it work. The good news is that God has created you for a specific purpose and has revealed the secrets that will help you find that purpose and make it succeed.

The secrets shared in the coming pages will guide you in understanding who you were created to be and how to put to use the gifts you've been given.

Secrets about Fulfilling Your Purpose

You Were Created for a Purpose

It is God who works in you to will and to act
according to his good purpose.

—Philippians 2:13 NIV

Have you ever wondered why you are here? I mean, really wondered, *why are you on the earth?* It is a good question, you know. Even when we run into a friend somewhere unexpected, we say, "So, what are you doing here?" There must be a reason, right? So we ask.

And no one ever says, "No reason. I just woke up this morning and was here at the mall. Could you tell me why I am here?" Unless they have amnesia, they know why they are there and what they are doing.

But, and this *is* amazing, as humans we *do* have amnesia a lot of times. Think about it. People just find themselves on the earth, wake up, and never ask the question "What am I doing here?" When you really think about it, that's pretty incredible. We know more about why we are at the mall than why we are alive on the earth and what our purpose is.

The "not knowing," the amnesia, is caused by a few things. One reason is that we have *forgotten* that we have a purpose. The whole human race has become disconnected from the original understanding that God created us and put us on the earth for a reason. Being so disconnected from him, we have just forgotten it. Each of us, personally. Amnesia. Just woke up here, and we don't remember why.

Another reason is that when you are in the mall, someone *asks* you why you're there. When your friend walks up and asks you, you answer. Otherwise, you don't think much about it; you just go about doing whatever you came to the mall to do. And so in life, if no one asks, we just go about our lives without ever thinking about the why—wandering through the mall with no purpose. The reality, though, is that Someone *is* asking. We are just too busy wandering around to hear.

And then the third reason is that in the absence of not knowing our purpose, we make one up. Or two, or several, which change with different seasons of life. I told you how I thought I knew what my life was about until I hit bottom. And then my purposes were taken away and I was lost. Other people do not lose their made-up purposes, but actually fulfill them, and then find that those purposes are not big enough to fill them up once they achieve them. Suicidal millionaires and drug-addicted movie stars prove that point.

So let's ask the question. "Why *are* you here?" And let me give you a suggestion of whom to turn to for the answer. I'm not suggesting that you emulate the latest gossip-magazine star to find your purpose in life. You won't find your purpose by following the best athletes on ESPN. The One you need to turn to is the person who made you. Your Creator. He is the reason you are here, and he has a purpose for your life.

> *Know that the Lord is God.*
> *It is he who made us, and we are his;*
> *we are his people, the sheep of his pasture.*[1]

OUT OF AMNESIA

The first thing to know about your purpose is that God is the reason for your existence. As the verse says, "Know that the Lord is God." That is the first thing we need to get straight if we are ever going to find our real purpose for life. He is the one, the reason that it is all here. We did not make ourselves. He made us. And because he did, we are not our own. We are his. We are his sheep, and wherever we hang out, it is *his* pasture. So, to find your purpose, begin by understanding that he created you to belong to him.

Next, understand that he created you for some reasons. First, he did it to have a relationship with you. He made you to love you. Much like parents who decide to have a child to love, raise, and relate to. It is all about the love he wants to share.

Then there's more. God did not just make you to be a blob sitting around with nothing to do. He gave you gifts and abilities. He wants you to put those abilities to use and multiply them in ways that serve *his* purposes, help other people, and fulfill you. He wants you to do good things of value with your life.

And he wants you to serve him directly. He wants you to volunteer for his army, and do whatever he needs done on the earth. He says that you are his arms, hands, and fingers on the planet, or at least your neighborhood. If he needs to get food to someone, he wants to dial your number and be able to make sure that it gets delivered. He has given you that awesome privilege of doing specific things on the earth that he has equipped you to do.

Also, and this is a cool one . . . he wants you to enjoy all of this! He did not make you as a slave facing drudgery. Many people feel like if they give themselves to God for his service, they are on the next boat for some jungle as a missionary. Tell that to the NBA players who are believers. They will laugh and tell you that they know that God has made them to play basketball and someone else to be a surgeon. Or as a young mother recently told me about raising her three young children, "I feel like I am doing what I was put on the earth to do." Bingo. She had found it, and she was not in a jungle somewhere.

But some people are. They gave themselves to God, and he did not send them to the NBA, the NFL, or to Mommy and Me. He sent them to a forsaken land to be missionaries. But here's the kicker—they say the same thing that the mother says or the NBA player says: they know that they are doing what they were made to do, and they are *thrilled* to be there, if they are where God wants them to be. They are in the sweet spot, his perfect will for them.

God wants you to enjoy your service to him, using your talents, celebrating life, and enjoying it all. As Solomon says,

> *I know that there is nothing better for men*
> *than to be happy and do good while they live.*
> *That everyone may eat and drink,*
> *and find satisfaction in all his toil—this is the gift of God.*[2]

God made life and work to be enjoyed.

THE STEP

So, now that we are awake and no longer have amnesia, what then? Solomon gives us another hint when he says to eat and drink and find satisfaction in work. He adds:

This too, I see, is from the hand of God,
for without him, who can eat or find enjoyment?[3]

In other words, the step we need to take is to stop wandering around in the mall as if we are on our own shopping spree and realize first things first. As Solomon points out, "without him" we will not find our purpose. We will keep wandering and not find enjoyment and fulfillment in our wanderings. We have to take the first step and surrender our lives to God, give our lives to him, and allow him to show us whether we should be in the NBA, nursery school, the operating room, or somewhere in a dark jungle. It comes with *surrender*.

Before you gag on that word, remember it this way: *he made you,* so he knows what he made you for. He knows better than you what is good for you. He wants the best for you, and he will lead you to it. Remember the verse above that says it was he who made us. Not ourselves. He knows, believe it or not, what is best for you even better than you do.

Remember my story? I was one of those who had to run my plan into the ground before I got it that he knew better and could guide me into what he made me for. Maybe you are there now. If you are, he can do it for you too. But hopefully you are not. You might even be doing well, wandering in the mall. If so . . . you get to just turn it all over to him because it is the smart thing to do, not because you have hit the wall. The main thing is to do it, no matter where you are today, winning or losing. He knows best.

Give up your life and trade it in for his. It will be better. Maybe not easier, but maybe it will be. It will not matter. It will be better. It may even look exactly like the one you have now, just with Someone other than you on the throne. Maybe nothing on the outside will change at all. Maybe some things will. Either way, if you are going to find your true purpose for being on the earth, it begins with turning it over to God. He will show you the most fulfilling life you can live, the one that was designed for you. But to find it, you have to give it up to him. Become his servant, and you will gain everything.

Jesus said it this way:

> *Whoever wants to save his life will lose it,*
> *but whoever loses his life for me will find it.*[4]

Once you do that—once you "lose your life"—he will guide you. You will still dream and have visions, even more than before. It becomes a relationship where God helps you achieve the things that you were created to do. You will make plans from your heart of hearts, and he will guide your steps. He will be your shepherd, and you will enjoy playing in his pasture. As Proverbs says,

> *In his heart a man plans his course,*
> *but the LORD determines his steps.*[5]

You will dream, and he will guide. Also, he will guide your dreams. The Shepherd will help you fulfill the purpose he has for you.

THE TWO GREAT COMMANDMENTS

When Jesus was asked about the greatest commandment, he said there were two: Love God with all your heart, mind, soul, and strength. And love your neighbor as yourself.[6]

That is a good way to summarize the beginning of this section on purpose. We will now look at several ways to succeed in whatever your purpose, dreams, and goals are as you embark on your journey with God. But all of them, in one way or another, come back to these two. Love him with all that you are, and you will find what to do and how to do it well. And when you do, whatever the specifics of that are, do them in ways that help others and do for them what you would want done for and to you. God bless you as you give it all to him, and get blessed a thousand times over as he gives your life back to you in ways that you could never have created for yourself. Because . . . it is he who has made us.

YOUR HEART DETERMINES THE COURSE OF YOUR LIFE

Guard your heart above all else,
for it determines the course of your life.

—PROVERBS 4:23 NLT

Rhonda Byrne had it partially right when she said in *The Secret,* "You become what you think about."[7] It is true that *much of what happens in our lives and relationships has its origins in our hearts and minds.* There is some truth to Byrne's idea that we create our own reality. Where the Judeo-Christian view would differ with Byrne is that ultimately God, not our own thoughts, is in control of the universe. Further, the relationship between our thoughts and our reality does not magically come about because the universe responds to the vibes we send out. We are not gods, and the universe does not obey our every command. (What would happen if you and I both send out vibes desiring the same parking space or we're positively pulling for opposing teams in the Super Bowl?) Rather, the relationship between thoughts and reality lies in the truth that *who we are on the inside creates much of our outside life.* As the ancient philosopher Heraclitus said, "A man's character is his destiny."

Tiger Woods's thoughts and vibes regarding his ability to make a putt to win the US Open will produce a very different result than mine. His inner world of how he thinks about the next shot has won many major championships. His inner world finds its way to the outside world; it moves from vision to reality, but it begins with vision. His vision—his thoughts about winning—began as a young child. Today we see the fruits of those thoughts.

YOU CAN KNOW A TREE BY ITS FRUIT

The Bible has a lot to say about how our insides affect our outsides, and one of the pictures it uses to show us how this works is a tree and its fruit:

> *By their fruit you will recognize them.*
> *Do people pick grapes from thorn bushes, or figs from thistles?*
> *Likewise every good tree bears good fruit,*
> *but a bad tree bears bad fruit.*
> *A good tree cannot bear bad fruit,*
> *and a bad tree cannot bear good fruit.*[8]

> *Make a tree good and its fruit will be good,*
> *or make a tree bad and its fruit will be bad,*
> *for a tree is recognized by its fruit.*[9]

You have seen this in life, I'm sure. A good tree, someone who is healthy, has healthy relationships, for example. And someone who is really dysfunctional on the inside tends to have dysfunctional relationships as well.

Who you are on the inside has everything to do with what your life looks like on the outside. I ran into a friend the other day whom I have known for about ten years, enough time to know his patterns. He was telling me about his new business venture. He was *so positive*. He was so certain that this one was going to be huge. It sounded great, but there was only one problem. I have heard his enthusiasm and certainty many times before, on many different deals, over several years. And they never pan out. He has never made it. Why? Lack of positive thinking? No, in fact, his thinking is too positive.

The reason he does not make it is because he lacks some key things "inside the tree," inside his character, that would produce the kind of fruit he is looking for. This is what keeps him from realizing the success he desires and that this new venture could actually afford him. Further, if it had been anyone else, I would probably have invested, because it sounded so solid and good. But I know him and a lot about his character—his tree—and I knew that no matter how good the deal or the opportunity, he will find a way for it not to work. That is just who he is.

This is one of the most important secrets God teaches us: one of the best things you can do for yourself is to work on *who you are as a person*. Until you do this, you will find ways to sabotage

> WHO YOU ARE ON THE INSIDE HAS EVERYTHING TO DO WITH WHAT YOUR LIFE LOOKS LIKE ON THE OUTSIDE.

147

the best jobs, the best relationships, the best opportunities, and just about everything else that comes your way. Not intentional sabotage, but the kind that comes when someone is not ready or able to do something.

Why is it that some people have a long line of successes and others a long line of failures? Sure, being in the right place at the right time, knowing the right people, etc. can all be factors. But the overriding truth is that the course of our lives has more to do with who we are as people than with what chances come our way. I see people who go through years of failed relationships, looking for the "right one"; but it never occurs to them that they need to *become* the right one in order to *attract* the right one. It never occurs to them that although God and life present us with opportunities and "chances," we make a lot of our own opportunities as well.

THE LAW OF SOWING AND REAPING

Another way that the Bible talks about our heart determining the course of our lives is through the law of sowing and reaping. When you look at it, the law of attraction in *The Secret* has some uncanny similarities to this law of God. Here's how it works: whatever you sow into yourself—like a new job skill or a new relationship skill—you will reap in better results at work and improved relationships.

Just look around you. Who gets the good jobs or develops the good career? Usually, the people who have developed their talents, experience, résumés, and abilities. They sowed career development into their lives and reaped the benefits. Who attracts the good people into relationships? The people who have worked out their relational issues. Who finds themselves healthy, and who is sick as a general rule? Generally speaking, people who sow healthy lifestyles reap health, and those whose lifestyles are unhealthy reap sickness. There is a reason that insurance companies ask people about lifestyle issues and that banks want to check credit records. Barring explainable circumstances, who they are as people determines the course of their lives. Stop hoping against hope and begin working on the personhood that will produce results in your life!

The law of sowing and reaping is one of the most powerful laws in the universe. As Solomon put it:

> Cast your bread upon the waters,
> for after many days you will find it again.[10]

In other words, what you put out there will return to you in kind.

GOD AND LIFE RISE UP TO MEET YOU WHERE YOU ARE

Another dimension to the law of sowing and reaping—and similar to the law of attraction—is that as we grow and get better and more equipped, we are met with new opportunities and situations that are the right fit to our new level of growth and ability. I have seen this time and time again in my own life as well as in the lives of others. As I have gained a new skill or ventured into some new arena, God opened doors, and the opportunities just somehow showed up. God brings those, the Bible teaches, as we are ready. There is an old proverb that says, "When the student is ready, a teacher will appear." The key is for you to be *ready*, to be working on yourself, so that God can bring you to the next step in your path of growth. As you are ready, the step will appear. As you get healthy, that healthy relationship will appear. As you get skilled, that job opportunity will show up. God directs our steps. We attract into our lives what we are ready for.

Over and over the Bible affirms the truth that God and life will respond to where you are.[11] He may even discipline you[12] out of his love for you. Sometimes *challenges* are exactly what you need to get to the next step. James says we are to actually "consider it all joy"[13] when we face trials, because sometimes they help us grow in some way. Sometimes challenges or difficulties bring about positive changes in us that make us ready for coming opportunities. By challenges and difficulties, I am not talking about abuse or mistreatment or tragedies that happen to people. These are not discipline, but hardships that you did not cause or need. But sometimes God does allow us to go through some other kinds of difficulty in order to grow our character, a kind of training. If you want to get to the next level, learn the lessons from the situation you are in so you won't have to repeat that grade!

WHAT'S AT YOUR HEART DETERMINES WHO YOU ARE

Research has shown that it is possible to predict the later academic success of five-year-olds by measuring certain character traits over and above IQ. When they followed five-year-olds long-term into high school and beyond, *how smart they were did not predict success as well as their ability to delay gratification!* The group that could delay gratification at age five outperformed kids who were smarter than them later on in high school but who lacked that character trait.

Other research has proven that optimism is a greater predictor of success in sales than industry tests of aptitude. If you have a heart and mind of pessimism, the course of your life will be very different from that of someone with a positive outlook. An alternate version of Proverbs 4:23 says, "Keep your heart with all diligence, for out of it spring the *issues of life.*"[14] This reading adds a whole new dimension to our understanding. The "issue" the optimistic sales person deals with is, "Where am I going to spend all this money I am making?" whereas the "issue of life" for the pessimist will be completely different because his heart is different. His mind-set will be more along the lines of "Where am I going to find work now? This sales thing is not working."

The Bible and life both show us that the kind of person you are determines what kind of life you "attract." The scriptures below are just a few more where God drives home the point that what's on the inside—our characters, our hearts, our minds, our souls—determines a lot of what happens in our lives. The correlations are amazingly obvious:

> *Careful words make for a careful life;*
> *careless talk may ruin everything.*[15]

> *No matter how much you want, laziness won't help a bit,*
> *but hard work will reward you with more than enough.*[16]

> *You are in for trouble if you sin,*
> *but you will be rewarded if you live right.*[17]

As you grow, God and life will reward your growth by giving you new opportunities and open doors. So here are some "inside the tree" things you might work on to prepare your heart for a life filled with purpose:

- gaining self-confidence

- overcoming fear

- gaining skills

- gaining wisdom and knowledge

- practicing persistence and perseverance

- changing attitudes about failure

- getting rid of bitterness

- stopping blame

- giving up victim thinking

- growing in your ability to confront

- overcoming control issues

- giving up and controlling anger

- gaining the ability to say no

- growing in relationship skills

- resolving old hurts and trauma

- overcoming depression

- overcoming addictions or compulsive behaviors

- overcoming impulsivity

- giving up wishful thinking

As you work on the "inside of the tree," or character growth, you will find that the outside picture begins to change as a result. Your life direction will take shape as the inside of you falls in line with God's purpose for you.

$\mathcal{W}$E ARE NOT ALL ALIKE

*In his grace, God has given us different gifts
for doing certain things well.*
—ROMANS 12:6 NLT

The research is in: when people do what they are good at, the results are better than when they don't. For a long time, since the days of the Bible, people have been aware that we are not all alike. *We all have different gifts and abilities.* And we all have different amounts and degrees of those gifts as well. Figuring out what those abilities are is one of the keys to living a purposeful life.

PIGS WITH PURPOSE

Finding out what you are good at—or have a natural or God-given ability to do well—is an important key to finding purpose in your life. As the old saying goes, "You can't teach a pig to sing. It frustrates the pig, and the music is bad." Many times, we try to do things that are not aligned with our passion and gifts. As a result, the music is bad, and we are not happy. But put a pig in the right job and he will succeed, just as long as he doesn't have to sing.

This is old wisdom from ages gone by. Nowadays, it is also science. Way back in the days of the Bible, when it was time to build the temple, for example, Solomon recruited the best build-ers from Tyre to build the amazing structure.[18] Today, corporations spend millions of dollars recruiting people who are good at what the jobs require, and then in making sure that the new hires are spend-ing their time doing the things they are good at. Scientific testing gives companies tools to find out what people are gifted in and what they are not.

The reason they do this is exactly what the Bible teaches: God has given people different gifts, abilities, talents, intelligence, skills, and the like.[19] We are all different, and the best companies have people spending their time in their gifts and out of their areas of weakness. Much research has shown that companies and individuals do the best when people are spending their time doing what they do well and avoiding what they do not do well.

SELF-DISCOVERY—THROUGH YOUR CREATOR'S EYES

These keys to finding out who God made you to be are outlined in the book of Romans, chapter 12, and in other places in the Bible. In that famous passage, we find some important steps to discover-ing God's will for you:

1. *Offer yourself to God for his use* (verse 1). Remember, the Bible says that God has an investment in you, so if you offer your-self to him, in his service, he has a plan for you that involves the way that he made you. As Rick Warren said in the first line of *The Purpose Driven Life*, "It is not about you." Ask God who he

made you to be and what he wants you to do. He will show you. Then commit your goals and work to him. Proverbs 16:3 NIV says, "Commit to the LORD whatever you do, and your plans will succeed." Start with him. He created you with success in mind.

2. *Do not be conformed to the outside world, allowing it to mold you into someone you are not* (verse 2). If you let the other people, the pressures of the culture, your family, or anyone else mold you into someone you are not, you will never find out who God created you to be. The verse says that, instead, you are to be "transformed by the renewing of your mind." Get God's ways into your thinking as we have been talking about in this book, and you will find your true self. Remember, not being conformed means that you have to say no to other people's definitions of you or what you ought to do. Listening to the counsel of those who know you is certainly important; but sometimes parents, family, friends, etc. try to make you into who *they* think you should be instead of who God made you to be. Do not be conformed; hang tough to be who you ought to be.

3. *Don't think more highly of yourself than you ought* (verse 3). You will never find out who you are if you have too high an opinion of yourself or unrealistic expectations for yourself. That does not mean you should not dream big. Of course you should. *But start at the level where you are.* If you someday want to be a CEO, fine. But for now, be the best worker, then the best manager, then the best V.P., and so on up the ladder. No one begins at the top. Be humble, be diligent, and do the best you can along the way.

The big positions will come as you do well in the little ones.

Plus, when your expectations of yourself are too high, you think you should be perfect and never fail. That is the kiss of death to success. Success *always* includes failure along the way. So do not think of yourself as perfect or as one who should not make mistakes. Accept your imperfections and mistakes, learn from them when they come, and then go on. Don't get down on yourself, as the noise of that will get in the way of figuring out who you really are.

4. *Use your gifts in proportion to the faith God has given you* (verses 6–8). Whereas you should not go overboard and expect too much, you also have to use what you are given. We will look more at this later in this section, but you will *never* find out who you are if you do not *step out and try things.* Try, try, try. The way to discover our passions and gifts is through experience. Get out there and find out how good you are, what you like, what you dislike, and what reality is. We know after we try, not before.

5. *Get feedback from counselors and coaches.* Remember that the best performers in the world get coaching and rely on counselors. As the wisdom of Proverbs tells us:

> *Refuse good advise and watch your plans fail;*
> *take good counsel and watch them succeed.*[20]

We need others—not to define us per se, but to see our gifts and validate them. Ask people you trust about your strengths and what they think they are, but make sure you ask people who have experience with you and know what they are talking about. And make sure they do not have their own agendas to make you someone you are not!

Continually pray for God's guidance and direction. Remember, he has promised to lead you. I like the way the psalmist puts it:

> Lead me by your truth and teach me,
> for you are the God who saves me.
> All day long I put my hope in you.
> Who are those who fear the LORD?
> He will show them the path they should choose.
> They will live in prosperity,
> and their children will inherit the land.[21]

God will guide you into your true gifts and abilities as you commit yourself to him.

6. *Listen to your heart.* God has made each of us with our own set of gifts and abilities. You know what you like and what you don't. What gives you energy and what burns you out? Listen to those things. What makes you come alive? The more time you can spend there, the better. Sometimes it's not possible for your passions and your job to connect. When that's the case, you can express your passions in other ways. But some people are able to make a career out of their passions. Whatever your situation,

always find a way to express your heart, either in work, play, or service to God and others. The apostle Paul was a tentmaker, and Jesus was a carpenter. But we know they spent a lot of time fulfilling their purpose outside of those arenas.

Finding your gifts is key to fulfilling your purpose. As you work from your true center, from who you really are, your life will come from your heart, and God will guide. Proverbs 16:9 (NIV) says, "In his heart a man plans his course, but the LORD determines his steps." Find your heart and your true gifts, then whether in your vocation or your avocation, hobbies, or service, set your heart on pleasing God first and expressing who you are second, and you will do well.

$\mathcal{W}$HATEVER YOU PUT TO USE WILL GROW

To those who use well what they are given,
even more will be given, and they will have an abundance.
But from those who do nothing,
even what little they have will be taken away.

—MATTHEW 25:29 NLT

I'm guessing that one of your arms is stronger and more developed than the other. Why? Because you *use it more than the other one.* You invest more effort in it, and it grows muscle as a result. The more you use it, the stronger it gets. Check out a dancer's legs sometime, and you will see what I mean. Or a bowler's forearm. What you put to use grows.

THE LAW OF "WHATEVER YOU PUT TO USE WILL GROW"

Are you beginning to get the sense that God has put some thought into how this universe is set up? That there really are some laws that govern not only things like gravity and motion but also how to make our lives work. Laws like the *law of sowing and reaping* and even the *law of attraction*, as we've defined it.

In the gospel of Matthew, Jesus tells a parable—a story about

Secrets about Your Purpo

three servants who were entrusted with some of their master's money while he was out of town on business. The master expected each of them to invest his money while he was gone, put it to good use, and give him a profitable return when he got back. Two of the servants invested their master's money and made a decent profit. These men benefited from the law of "whatever you put to use will grow." They understood that the parts of yourself and your life that you invest in and use *grow*, but the parts you don't use tend to wither, or atrophy. The master was so pleased with their results that he gave them authority over more things. The third man, however, did not fare so well.

THE LAW OF "USE IT OR LOSE IT"

As we look at the third man in Jesus's story, we are introduced to another law of life—a close cousin to the law of *whatever you put to use will grow*—that works just as predictably as the others we've talked about. The old saying "use it or lose it" could be lifted right from the end of the story of the three men and the talents. When called to give an account for how he'd handled the money he'd been given, this is the conversation that went down:

> "Master, I knew you were a harsh man, harvesting crops you didn't plant and gathering crops you didn't cultivate. I was afraid I would lose your money, so I hid it in the earth. Look, here is your money back."
>
> But the master replied, "You wicked and lazy servant! If

you knew I harvested crops I didn't plant and gathered crops I didn't cultivate, why didn't you deposit my money in the bank? At least I could have gotten some interest on it."

Then he ordered, "Take the money from this servant, and give it to the one with the ten bags of silver."[22]

What always stands out to me in this story is that in the areas where we feel afraid, we do the least. We hide to protect ourselves and do not step out and try. But we might discover that we actually *do* have some abilities or resources in these areas if we tried. We might find that if we would just use them, they would multiply. The two people in the story who were rewarded were the ones who took what they were given and did something with it. They invested themselves.

But when we are afraid, we do what the third person did. We see all the things that can go wrong, we think the outside world is going to get us in some way, and we become even more fearful. We also tend to blame our inactivity on others or the company or the boss or the economy or the customer or *anything* but our own inactivity.

A Tale of Two Businessmen

Not long ago I ran into a guy who had been talking about making a change in his work and dreams for quite a while but always seemed to have some excuse for not doing it. He never did step out and try anything, for one reason or another. He really wanted to do something in real estate and in some related areas, but there was always a reason not to make a move—literally for years. This particular time he was saying, "Well, the problem is that you can't do that without a lot of money, and I don't have enough to invest and get started." (Poor me.)

Then, right after talking to him, I had lunch with a friend who was telling me about his venture that was a few years old, and it was such a cause for celebration. Its value was now in the millions and millions, and all of his effort was paying off. Here is the interesting part . . . he had begun when he was in bankruptcy! Not only did he have no money, *he had no ability to borrow any money.*

But what he also did not have was the other guy's fear, laziness, blaming, excusing, and all the other reasons to not get moving and make something happen. So he found a deal, went out, got investors, and made it work. He

IN THE AREAS
WHERE WE FEEL
AFRAID, WE DO
THE LEAST.

did not need money to make money. He just needed to invest his great talent of evaluating deals and putting them together. It's a lot better to have bankruptcy and the right mind-set than to be solvent but stuck in the mud of your own victim mentality.

Both men were very smart, and both had ample opportunity and availability to information, markets, and the like. Both had deal-making capacities. The difference was that one took what he had and went into action and the other didn't. The successful man invested himself in the real world and got real-world results.

MAKING IT WORK

This law is true in any area of life. If you want a relationship to work, invest yourself in it and it will grow. If you don't invest yourself in the relationship, it won't grow. It's that simple. Don't just gripe about the other person, but grow from your side of things, and the relationship will feel the effects. If you want your kids to do well, invest yourself in them, and they will do much better.

In order to find your purpose in life and determine how you will serve God and mankind, you have to do the same thing. Stop fantasizing, dig up your talent, and put it to use. When you do, the law of multiplication begins to kick in and things will grow.

The Magic of Multiplication

Investment is not linear. It is multiplicative. When you put money to use and invest the profits and dividends, you begin to get the magic of compounded interest. That is also what happens when you use your talents and abilities. You step out in an area and get involved; and as you get better, bigger opportunities come your way that have even greater return. But it all comes from taking that first step.

So, What's the First Step for You?

I was talking about this one day with a guy on an airplane, and he shared with me the story of his mother-in-law, whom he said exemplified stepping out, digging up a talent, and watching it multiply. He said that she became an actress at eighty! She had always wanted to do it, and finally she did. Slowly she began to get more and more parts and has been in lots of films and television shows as a result of stepping out, even at a time in life when most would have given up. But look at the multiplication! She did not let the excuses or what might or might not be possible stop her. She did it.

Get rid of the thinking that you have to conquer the world in the first step, and just take a little one. No one is asking you to change career fields, move to L.A., and become an actor! But if you have a passion, why not call the local community college and take one course? Why not get a coach and try to learn that sport you have always dreamed of? Big dreams do not become reality in big steps, but in a million little ones. How do you eat an elephant? One bite at a time. How do you build a career? By digging up your abilities and taking one little step at a time. How do you develop a fulfilling hobby? One little lesson at a time, or one little class, or one little try. Use it, and it will multiply.

Whatever you use, grows. What you don't, won't. Your purpose is waiting for you.

*W*HOLEHEARTED EFFORTS BRING REAL RESULTS

> *In all that he did in the service of the Temple of God*
> *and in his efforts to follow God's laws and commands,*
> *Hezekiah sought his God wholeheartedly.*
> *As a result, he was very successful.*
> —2 CHRONICLES 31:21 NLT

When the cook said that ham and eggs were going to be on the menu, the chicken and the pig had very different reactions. "I don't think you understand," the pig said to the chicken. "For me, this involves a very different level of commitment." And so it does. The pig had to give it all for that meal to happen.

Have you ever thought about what your "ham and eggs" is? Where are you the pig? What things in your life involve your "whole heart"? What do you want to succeed in so much that you are willing to put in all of who you are? That is what this secret is about. The things we want to succeed at require our full commitment; if we do not give it, they will flounder or will not realize their full potential. This is true in our relationships, our business dealings, our careers, our spiritual growth, and most important, in our relationship with God. Where we put our efforts, we see results.

Secrets about Your Purpose

Wholehearted Efforts Reap Whole Fruit

I have a friend who is a renowned heart and vascular surgeon. He is a leader in the field and is one of those people who not only practices latest techniques, but develops them. He is the kind of surgeon who does those insane procedures like running the blood out of the body, lowering the temperature to suspend the patient's metabolism, repairing the vessels, putting the blood back in, and warming the patient back up. Way-out-there stuff, "before it was fashionable," as they say. He has done very well in his profession. But you probably could have guessed that. He was a college room-mate of mine, and I remember when he decided that he was going to be a doctor. It was a whirlwind of the wholehearted kind.

He had been a business major, but in his sophomore year, he decided to change to pre-med. When he did, he pursued it with everything in him. Up every morning at 5 a.m., doing catch-up in the sciences, making flash cards to learn the equations for organic chemistry, hitting the books until late at night when others were out partying. In the summer, he got jobs in hospitals to tighten up the résumé for admission into med school. He read about medicine in his spare time, and on and on. You could tell his heart was in it. And the fruit of his wholeheartedness is evident today.

The Divine Spark in You

There are a lot of really cool things about being created in God's image.[23] One of those is that he has passed on to us the ability to will things and bring them into fruition. I would say that's pretty amazing. One thing about God is that whatever he "wills," or desires, ultimately comes to pass. And why is that? Besides the fact that he has the *ability* to make it happen, it is because he wants it with all his heart. You don't see unfinished things floating around the universe that he just never got around to because his "heart was not in it." What he desires, he desires with all of him, and he makes it happen. And here is the secret: Although you don't have omnipotent will like God, you do have the ability to make things happen—when you desire things that line up with his will and when you put your whole heart into them. Because you "share in God's divine nature."

But if we are halfhearted in our pursuits, we will only get halfway—if that far.

HALFHEARTED RESULTS

I got a call on the radio from a woman who was trying to decide whether to stay with her boyfriend. She said that the relationship was "serious" and that they were thinking about getting married. She also said she loved him very much and that they had been together for a couple of years. When I asked her what the problem was, she told me she found out he had cheated on her and that she did not feel like she was a priority to him. She felt as if he cared a lot more about his work than he did about her. So she was bummed because she wanted more from him than he was giving.

Then she said something interesting: "But I know he loves me."

I had no way of disputing that. But there was something I could say that I knew was right. "Maybe he does, but don't you want someone who loves you with his whole heart?"

That is when she got it. She saw that she was getting "half-hearted" love, and that would never be enough. So she moved on. Why? Because halfhearted results will never fulfill.

Another woman called the radio; she was struggling with whether or not she would be able to trust her husband after a sex addiction had wrecked their relationship. He was saying that he was not going to act out anymore, that he was sorry, and that he was now going to be fully committed to her and to getting better. But her dilemma was "How can I know whether or not to trust him. I want to, but how can I know?"

> IF WE ARE HALF-HEARTED IN OUR PURSUITS, WE WILL ONLY GET HALFWAY—IF THAT FAR.

I told her she did not need to be in a quandary about whether or not to trust him. To be in the position of judge—going back and forth, wondering all the time—would not be a good place for her to be.

So I asked her: "Do you think Peyton Manning has to talk people into trusting him to play football?" No, of course not. People trust him because of what they see, and it is the same thing with her husband. What she needed to see from him was wholeheartedness in pursuing recovery. I put it to her this way: "Look. This is kind of simple. If he is wholehearted about his recovery, you will not have to figure it out. You will see it. He will go to his meetings, pursue counseling, be figuring out his issues, pursue health and God on his own, etc., etc. He will be so hungry in his pursuit of getting well that you will not have to push him, nag him, wonder about him, or anything else. He will be a machine in motion, chasing after health with his whole heart. If you see this whirlwind of activity around getting better and pursuing a relationship with you, what will you have to decide about? You will know. You will see it. Wholeheartedness will do it for you."

And if he pursues wellness that way, he will find it. "Seek and you will find, knock and the door will be opened to you."[24] But halfhearted effort is nowhere.

If you go after what you want with only a "mixed heart," you will get mixed results. If your whole heart is not in something, you start and stop, you pull back when there are obstacles, you don't invest the resources you need to invest, you slow down when you are afraid or things get hard, and you generally do not gain the confidence of those you need as allies. So if you want something and you want it bad enough to pursue it, make sure you pursue it with all that you are.

THE WAY IT WORKS

At the very center of the way it works is God. I love the above description of Hezekiah that says, "He sought his God and worked wholeheartedly. And so he prospered."[25] Those are the two tracks that his prosperity rested on: (1) wholeheartedness in seeking God, and (2) wholeheartedness in working at whatever he put his hands to. If you do both of these, then you will be on the same track.

If you are going to have good results—in your relationship with God, with others, with a spouse, or with a family member—you are going to have to give your heart to it. Your whole heart. *That is the way it works.* If you are going to get great results in a sport or a business or a skill or in recovery from an addiction or emotional problem, you are going to have to give your heart to it. Your whole heart. *That is the way it works.*

The "greats" in life give themselves totally to becoming the ham of ham and eggs. Great athletes practice and give themselves totally to their sport. People with great families do not play around at being mothers and fathers, husbands and wives. They give themselves totally to the relationships. That's the way it works. And the good thing is that *it works.*

WHAT KEEPS IT FROM WORKING

If working with your whole heart brings success, then why don't we do it? Here are some reasons you may need to look at:

- *Fear of failing.* You want to win, but you're afraid you might fail, so you hold back.

- *Past hurt that blocks passion.* You carry around old pain, and you cannot feel your energy to pursue something new.

- *Discouragement from the past.* You've been put down or lost before, and you feel beaten before you start, so your whole heart is not available to you.

- *Mixed motives.* You want the goal, but you want it for another reason besides the goal itself, so your heart is not really in the pursuit, but in it for the money, acclaim, status, or something else that is not pure.

- *Conflict over the goal itself.* You want it, but you want something else too, or you want it and don't want it at the same time.

- *Shackled by someone else's control.* You want your goal, but you are pulled away because someone else has control over your time and energy too.

- *Feelings of inadequacy.* Your lack of confidence in yourself causes so much doubt that you cannot move forward wholeheartedly.

- *Incompatible wishes.* You want two things at the same time that are incompatible—e.g., you want to be married and have a family, and you want ultimate freedom and control over your time and life.

- *Undefined passions.* You have never found your real passion that would cause you to be the ham.

If you recognize yourself in any of the above, get before God and with one or two or three people you trust, and get to the bottom of what is holding you back. Give all of yourself to God and to your dreams, and the power of both of these will make your heart like Hezekiah's, or Solomon's when he built the temple. God blesses the wholehearted.

ONE WOMAN'S HAM

Jesus told a parable about a woman who sought justice with her whole heart, as an example of how we should approach God:

> In a certain town there was a judge who neither feared God nor cared about men. And there was a widow in that town who kept coming to him with the plea, "Grant me justice against my adversary."
>
> For some time he refused. But finally he said to himself, "Even though I don't fear God or care about men, yet because this widow keeps bothering me, I will see that she gets justice, so that she won't eventually wear me out with her coming!"[26]

This was her ham—this woman put her whole heart into getting what she needed from the judge; through persistence and diligence she pressed her case on him—and he finally gave her what she wanted just to get her to shut up. Making people sick of us isn't the only tool we have for getting what we need, but this poor woman's persistence was commended by Jesus.

So, what is your ham? What do you want bad enough to be like this woman? Or like my surgeon friend? If it allows you to keep God at your very center and you pursue it with your whole heart, no one will have to guess whether or not you can be trusted with it. Not even God.

We conclude with the most powerful secrets of all—secrets about God himself. You've seen him on every page of this book, and now we will move in for a closer view. This God, who created you and the entire universe, is deeply attracted to you. He cares for you so much that he actually left heaven and became one of us.

He wants to relate to you in a real and intimate way. And to do that, he has told us some secrets about himself so that we may experience him—and life—in the way it was intended.

Secrets about God

THE GOD OF THE UNIVERSE WANTS A PERSONAL RELATIONSHIP WITH YOU

O LORD, you have searched me and you know me.
You know when I sit and when I rise;
you perceive my thoughts from afar.
You discern my going out and my lying down;
you are familiar with all my ways.
Before a word is on my tongue
you know it completely, O LORD.

—PSALM 139:1–4 NIV

John Gottman is one of the premier researchers on marriage and relationships. In his lab, he has videotaped zillions of hours of couples interacting, and as a result has quantified the ingredients that lead to lasting marriages and those that lead to divorce. According to his research, by watching couples interact, he can predict which ones will divorce with a 91 percent accuracy. Pretty impressive. But when you read what his predictions are based on, it all begins to make sense. Here is an example:

He notes that when he observes couples, much of what they talk about is not big drama or earth-shattering topics, but little, seemingly meaningless chitchat. Here's what he says:

> You might think I'd find viewing hour after hour of such scenes unbearably boring. On the contrary: When couples engage in lots of chitchat like this, I can be pretty sure that they will stay happily married. What's really happening in these brief exchanges is that the husband and wife are connecting—they are turning toward each other. In couples who go on to divorce or live together unhappily, such small moments of connection are rare. More often the wife doesn't look up from her magazine—and if she does, her husband doesn't acknowledge what she says.[1]

It's not in the mountaintop experiences that long-term relationships are built but in the moment-to-moment connectedness of simply sharing life together. That is one of the keys to lasting relationships of any kind.

And that is exactly what God wants from us as well. He can create all the mountaintop experiences with us that he desires, and sometimes he does. Most people of faith can point to a time or two when they've had some encounter with God that was out of the ordinary. But they will all tell you that those times are the rare exceptions. The rest of their relationship with him is built on the little day-to-day connections, the kind of chitchat connections that Gottman observes in healthy marriages. As you simply share with God the things that are in your heart and on your mind, you will grow deeper and closer in relationship with him.

THE CREATOR HAS A THING FOR YOU

What an amazing concept. The Creator of the Universe wants an intimate relationship with you. He desires it. He wants you to share all of your thoughts, feelings, cares, dreams, fears, and everything else with him. Look at just a few of the scriptures that tell us how God feels about us.

He knows you. The Psalm 139 passage quoted at the beginning of this section says that God spends focused attention on you. He knows all about you. He attends to you when you sit down and when you rise up, going out and lying down. Everything you do, big or small, he is interested in.

He cares for you. In the book of 1 Peter, we read, "Cast all your anxiety on him because he cares for you,"[2] and the psalmist says, "Cast your cares on the LORD and he will sustain you."[3]

He wants you to call him "Abba." I think this is one of my favorite verses about God's love for us, because *Abba* is the word for "Papa"—not the formal Father, not even Dad, but the affectionate, intimate term Papa.[4] He is a papa who wants you to take everything to him and to be more intimate with him than with anyone in your life, because he knows you inside and out and cares infinitely for you.

He wants you to "remain" or "abide" in him. This means to be one with him, in an intimate love relationship just as Jesus is with God: "As the Father has loved me, so have I loved you. Now remain in my love."[5] The Greek word translated "remain" means to "abide" or "dwell." This is not a once-a-week-on-Sunday "checking in" with God or when we're in trouble asking him for a rescue. It is dwelling with, living with, being with, all of the time. That is the kind of relationship he wants with us.

GOD'S ATTRACTION TO US

The God of the Bible is not some far-off judge or distant, wrathful God. He is a father who wants you to take everything to him and be more intimate with him than with anyone else in your life.

We would agree with *The Secret* that there is a powerful attraction in the universe. But the attraction talked about in that book is with an impersonal, unfeeling universe. It doesn't really care about you—or anything else for that matter—one way or the other. It just is. Sort of like the Force in *Star Wars*, but not even that personal. Even the Force was something that could be with you. When it comes to the impersonal universe, there isn't even a with.

But the God of the Bible is *very* personal and *longs* to be with us. So be with him. Talk to him, all through the day. Talk to him about what you are thinking, feeling, wanting, not wanting. Talk to him about your frustrations or the things you think are funny. Talk to him when you are scared or trying to figure something out. When I notice something about life or a person or a situation or myself that perplexes me, one of my favorite things to do is to just say, "God help me with that," or, "God, show me about that."

> TALK TO HIM ABOUT YOUR FRUSTRATIONS OR THE THINGS YOU THINK ARE FUNNY.

And then I just let it go. So many times, sometimes a long time later, the answer will come.

Abide in him, for it is the only way to a great relationship—and it is a relationship with a great promise from Jesus:

> *If you remain in me and my words remain in you,*
> *ask whatever you wish, and it will be given you.*[6]

As we become more and more "one" with him, his will and ours become more united. As that happens, the things we want will be the things that he wants for us, and they will happen.

Respond to God's desire for intimacy with you—and you're gonna love it.

GOD IS FOR YOU, NOT AGAINST YOU

He will take great delight in you,
he will quiet you with his love,
he will rejoice over you with singing.

—ZEPHANIAH 3:17 NIV

Did you know that God is happy when you do well? Just like a father who wants his children to do well, God wants you to do well too. That, by the way, is one of the reasons that the secret of trusting him makes so much sense. For you to trust him and really depend on him for your dreams, you need to believe that *God is for you, not against you,* and that he actually *wants* good things for you.

A NEW OUTLOOK

Research shows us that people's success depends greatly on their *outlook,* their view of the world. It also depends on their view of God. Just look around and you'll see this is true. People who believe that God is for them take bold steps toward their pursuits and goals. But people who think God or life is against them hold back—always afraid to take the next step and never going anywhere.

Secrets about God

A NEW KIND OF TOMORROW

Have you ever felt like you were working against the system? You might be trying, for example, to get to the next level in your job or your company, and it seems that at every turn some obstacle gets in your way and you just can't move forward. Or when you were growing up, maybe you had a teacher or a coach who always seemed to be picking on you.

For some, it seems that life is somehow lined up against them, poised at every juncture to make sure that good things do not ultimately materialize. Maybe you can identify with some of these scenarios:

- You were really interested in someone you were dating, but he or she broke up with you. You began to feel like, "I will never have a good relationship. It happens for other people, but not for me."

- You have been stuck in an emotional issue or a behavior problem or addiction for some time, and you feel as if it will never get better.

- You have a goal or a dream that you want to materialize, but for some reason, it seems that no matter where you turn, nothing works out.

There are lots of reasons people get bogged down in this kind of thinking. Sometimes, their life experiences teach them that

183

to hope for something good is just a fantasy. Their dreams have never come true in the past, so there's no reason to believe that tomorrow will be any different. They *want* a different kind of life but have difficulty believing that it could ever happen. That is understandable . . . *unless* . . . *unless there is Someone very powerful who wants you to make it*—Someone who has the desire *and* ability to bring it about for you.

That is exactly what the Bible says is true for those who are in relationship with God. He is for you, he wants to make good things happen for you, and he is powerful enough to do something about it.

When you know that God is for you, you will be able to go through any obstacles or failures in a powerful way. You will depend on him, even when it seems that all is lost or that everyone else is against you.

You need to know this: you are not the only one who wants good things for you. God wants it even more than you do. He will never do anything to harm you; everything he does will be to help you and for your good.[7]

GOD WANTS YOU TO SUCCEED

Two of the things God created you to do especially well are to *love others* and to use the *talents and abilities* he gave you for his purposes. So if he went to all this trouble to create you this way, he is all for your success in these areas. It is his design, and he will not work against himself.

We all desire to have good relationships, and we all desire to use our talents and abilities in ways that make a contribution. God has given us more than enough opportunities to do all of this. He has given us all kinds of relationships through which we can love and serve each other, and he has delegated the work of the whole earth to humans to accomplish. When we use the love and talents he put in us in meaningful ways, his purposes are accomplished. What he has given us can produce all "varieties" of fruit: spiritual, material, relational, and more.

The Bible actually calls us "God's workmanship":

> We are God's workmanship,
> created in Christ Jesus to do good works,
> which God prepared in advance for us to do.[8]

Workmanship means "product of a skilled artisan." In other words, you are the handcrafted product of God, the skilled artisan, who made you for his specific purposes. So when you want to succeed at things that align with his purposes for you, you can be assured that your desires are not just a bunch of empty wishes but are plans that God has for you that he himself created.

If an NFL owner drafts a player for his team, he *wants that player to succeed.* If you are on God's team, God wants you to succeed too. He did not create you to fail. He desires your success so much that he will be actively involved in helping you do the things he has made you to do. If you delight in him, he wants to give you what you desire:

> *Take delight in the LORD,*
> *and he will give you your heart's desires.*[9]

So many people feel that God looks down on them for having dreams and desires and will do nothing to help them. This is just not true. God *longs* to fulfill the desires of our hearts when we live according to his will. When you want to succeed in some area, know that God is *for* you.

WHAT DOES IT MEAN WHEN IT DOESN'T WORK OUT?

What if you really are trying to live according to God's will and are walking in relationship with him, but your dreams still don't come true? Does that mean that God is really not for you, after all? Or maybe that he is not powerful enough to help? No, it does not mean either. Here are some things that may be going on:

Sometimes we want something that is not best for us. We may think it is "in God's will," but in reality, what we want might bring us harm. If you are a parent, you know there are things your children want that are not best for them, and so you say no, because you are for them. The *not* granting of the wish is the best thing you could do for them. Sometimes the reason things don't work out the way we want them to is because God cares too much to give us what we want.

We may not be ready for what we ask for. We may not get exactly what we want exactly when we want it because we are not "there" yet in our growth process. We may not be ready for that success yet. Dating relationships are a good example of this. It may take a few painful relationships for people to figure out who they need to be or the kind of person they need to find in order to have something that lasts. Or the false starts we experience in our career path may be the training steps God is using to get us there.

Sometimes others use their free will to harm us. Bad people may hurt us and derail us from getting where we want to go or accomplishing what we want to accomplish. That is not God's doing, but people's. Every one of us—you, me, everyone—has the free will to do good or evil, to harm others or be kind, to lie, care, steal, or hurt. You can bet that God hurts when someone hurts you. But it is not God who is to blame any more than parents are to blame if a playmate at school hurts their child. When we give our children freedom, they sometimes get hurt. Though the parents are not to blame, they are always there to help when the child is hurt.

Our desire for things may come from unhealthy motives. If our goal is simply to fill our ego or our materialism or our greed, then God is probably not going to contribute to making us sicker than we already are. As James says, sometimes we ask but do not receive because our motives are wrong.[10]

Sometimes we simply haven't asked. God wants to give good gifts to us, but he also wants us to ask him. James speaks to us again: "You do not have, because you do not ask God."[11]

But even in outcomes that are not what we desire, God is always there, and he is always for you. He is not a magic genie—as some would have us believe—nor is he the room-service delivery person who gives us everything we want. The Bible does not speak of a universe that supplies us with whatever we want as long as we send out the right thoughts. It speaks of a God who, just like any good parent, fulfills some of our desires but not all. Sometimes parents require that children give up what they want for the greater purposes of the family. Sometimes parents want the child to work instead of play, and no matter how hard the child wishes, the loving parent sometimes says, "It's not about you today. Today you are on a larger agenda." But the good parent always has a good reason and an agenda that in the end is going to be good for the child as well.

Our Father God is the most perfect parent of all. You can trust that he will consistently be for you.

Always remember and live out this truth:

If God is for us, who can be against us?[12]

Secrets about Go

GOD DOES NOT WANT YOU TO FEEL GUILTY

> *Though your sins are like scarlet,*
> *I will make them as white as snow.*
> *Though they are red like crimson,*
> *I will make them as white as wool.*
>
> —ISAIAH 1:18 NLT

For many people, God and guilt go together. Whether it was their religious upbringing, their church, or their own musings about God, they have a strong association between the two. So whenever they think about God, they feel some sort of guilt or shame, as if he is not pleased with them, as if in his eyes they need to do better.

DOES GUILT REALLY MOTIVATE US TO DO BETTER?

Some people have a misunderstanding about guilt. They think it is a good thing, that it somehow motivates them to do better. So . . . if they do something bad or do not live up to the expectations of God or others, they see guilt as the motivation that will turn them around and make them behave differently. They think if they feel bad enough about something, they will change. Unfortunately, they not only apply this theory to themselves, but to others. They will often make someone else feel bad, hoping to change the person's behavior. It's the old "in the doghouse" plan.

But the reality is, guilt doesn't work all that well. And more important than that, God does not want you to feel guilty. In fact, he does not want it so badly that *he died on the cross to forgive you of anything you have done or ever will do so that you will never have to suffer from feelings of condemnation ever again.* As the verse at the beginning of this section says, he wants you to feel as white as snow, with no stains of guilt anywhere on your soul. He knows that people who are not burdened by guilt and shame are free to be the best they can be.

THE REALITY IS, GUILT DOESN'T WORK ALL THAT WELL.

And besides that, guilt actually gets in the way of your becoming better. It does not change you long-term; it only slows you down. Your guilty spouse does not become a more loving spouse because you made him or her feel bad. The guilt an addict feels never breaks the cycle; rather, it pushes him or her into another episode to escape how bad he feels. Guilt is part of the problem, not the solution.

The answer is simple, and the answer is total forgiveness. No strings attached, nothing to do to deserve it except to accept it. That is the forgiveness God provides, no matter what you might have heard. That kind of forgiveness leads to freedom from your past and all your failures, and it sets you free to have a very different kind of future.

MISCONCEPTIONS ABOUT GOD

I was getting into my car to go to church one morning when a neighbor stopped and asked where I was headed. "Going to church. Want to come?"

"Are you joking?" she said. "No way!"

"Why not?" I asked.

"Can't handle the guilt. I have enough of my own without going to church to get more."

"Okay," I said. "But I would love to hear about that sometime."

She waved good-bye, and I could see that she had few second thoughts about my offer.

As I drove to church, I began to think about something: how in the world did the institution (the church), which was started by someone (Jesus) who said that he came to the earth to abolish guilt, become the Wal-Mart of guilt? How is that possible? Why do people feel like a relationship with God automatically includes guilt? Jesus's purpose couldn't be further from this impression:

> *God did not send his Son into the world*
> *to condemn the world,*
> *but to save the world through him.*[13]

There are two important things in that verse for you to hear. The first is that he did not come to pronounce you guilty, judge you or condemn you. That is not his goal. He came to forgive, exactly the opposite of guilt. And every time he relates to you, that is how he looks at you if you have accepted him as Savior. Every time, no exceptions.

The second involves the word *save*. We know that he came to save us from punishment, separation from God, and hell. But there's more. That word *save* actually means to "heal" or "make whole." Listen to it this way: "I did not come to make you feel bad about your failures. I came to help you overcome them and get past them. I came to heal whatever is broken that keeps tripping you up, not shame you for it."

THE TRUTH ABOUT GOD

Here's a question: why would anyone *not* want to run to a God who offers 100 percent forgiveness and acceptance and helps us overcome our failures? There are a lot of reasons: like, being told he is *not* accepting and forgiving or that you have to fulfill a bunch of requirements before you can be forgiven. These misconceptions are taught every day, in churches and neighborhoods everywhere, just like they were in the days of the Bible. In fact, much of the New Testament was written to combat the thinking that God requires performance rather than believing and receiving. People just cannot believe the truth about God—that he offers forgiveness to all who will receive it. But it's true:

> *Everyone who believes in him receives*
> *forgiveness of sins through his name.*[14]

Secrets about God

Therefore there is now no condemnation
for those who are in Christ Jesus.[15]

"No condemnation." Zero. None. If you believe in him as your Savior, your guilt is gone, forever. As hard as it is for you to believe that, it is true. That is what the Bible says over and over. God's mission when he came to earth was to pronounce you "not guilty" because of him.

Why does God want you to be free from guilt?

Well, first of all because *he loves you and wants to be reconciled to you.* Just like in any relationship, if you are estranged from someone because you hurt him, you have to be forgiven of the wrong that is separating you in order for you to feel close again. God wanted us back. He wanted to have an intimate relationship with us, and that required reconciliation.

But there's more. *He wants you to become all that you were meant to be.* And you will never be all that you can be if your past or present failure is bringing you down. You will be burdened by it, feel unlovable, fearful, ashamed to let people know you, and will not be free. God wants you to be free of all that and be who he created you to be.

THE PROBLEM WITH GUILT

One of the biggest problems with guilt is that it gets in the way of seeing the reality of what you need to work on.

I once worked with a young woman who was sleeping around. After each incident, knowing it was wrong, she would vow never to let it happen again. But then she would meet some guy who seemed nice, and he would pressure her for more than she wanted to give, and . . . she would not be able to say no. Afterward, like most guys who push women for sex where there is no commitment, he would soon be gone. She would feel cheap, used, but mostly guilty.

"I know God says I shouldn't be doing this," she would say. "And each time, I think I won't, but I do. I hate myself. I am such a loser. What kind of Christian am I?"

The biggest consequence—that she was aware of—was her guilt. What consumed her was how "bad" she was. And that is the big problem with guilt. Her guilt was so strong and pervasive that it was all she could see. It blinded her to the real consequences of her behavior.

Her real problem was what was going on in her life while she was wasting time feeling guilty. Her real problem was that all the while, her heart was getting more and more split inside as she kept giving her body to guys who were not connected to her heart and soul. The division inside her psyche was getting stronger. She was losing the ability to even know what she felt for a guy she was with, as she detached from herself more and more.

On top of that, she was letting her dependency on these guys' attention rule her, all the while not developing the discernment and relationship skills needed to find someone who would be good for her long-term—the kind of guy who would be worth giving herself to. The real problems of her behavior were a combination of what *was* happening to her and what was *not* happening while she was caught in the cycle. Those were the things that I wanted her to see. But until the guilt was out of the way, she couldn't.

If we want to know how Jesus feels about someone like this, caught up in a sin, we find a graphic picture in John 8. Self-righteous Pharisees dragged a woman from the bed of a man she wasn't married to (these men managed to overlook the fact that there was also a guilty man in bed with her), and they literally threw her at Jesus's feet just to see how he would react. Besides confronting the men who wanted to stone her with his famous line, "If any one of you is without sin, let him be the first to throw a stone at her,"[16] he also had words for the woman caught in the act. Here's how their conversation went:

> *"Woman, . . . has no one condemned you?"*
> *"No one, sir," she said.*
> *"Then neither do I condemn you," Jesus declared.*
> *"Go now and leave your life of sin."*[17]

No condemnation. No heaping on of guilt. Just a simple instruction to leave sin behind. And notice the order: first the no-condemnation, then the life-instruction.

The woman I knew responded to Jesus's love much like the woman thrown at Jesus's feet. As I convinced her that although she felt guilty she was not condemned in God's eyes but totally loved and accepted,[18] she was able to lose the guilt. When it was gone, she felt lighter, "clean" was how she put it. And soon after realizing she was not condemned, she woke up. "You know . . . I am wrecking myself. If I don't figure this out, I am going to be a mess for the rest of my life." Bingo. God had begun to save, or heal, her once the condemnation was out of the way.

And a big part of getting that condemnation out of the way was the fact that she was talking it out with me and a few friends. She was getting her sin into the light, where it lost its power. David says that when he was silent about his sin, his "bones wasted away."[19] Most of the time, we need the love and acceptance of others to fully realize God's love.

BETTER THAN GUILT—GODLY SORROW

Is there such a thing as good guilt? No, not the emotion of guilt. But so many people try to distinguish between false guilt and true guilt, saying that true guilt is a good thing, because it helps you be aware of what you have done wrong so you'll change. It seems they are afraid that if you don't feel guilty, you will run around like a sociopath, not feeling anything as a result of your sin—like, no biggie.

Nothing is further from the truth. The Bible does say that when we do wrong—like the woman who was sleeping around—we should feel something negative—it's just not guilt. So, if we are not to feel guilty, what are we to feel? The Bible is clear about what you should feel, and any psychologist will tell you that feeling this will change your life. Not guilty, but *sorry*. When we do wrong, we should feel sorry. Sorry, like the woman felt. Sad and sorry that she was wasting her life and heart. She felt loss. And as she felt what she was losing by continuing in that pattern, she began to get the proper motivation to change, something guilt could never give her. Listen to how the apostle Paul compares this kind of sorrow with the guilt of the world:

> *Godly sorrow brings repentance that leads*
> *to salvation and leaves no regret,*
> *but worldly sorrow brings death.*
> *See what this godly sorrow has produced in you:*
> *what earnestness, what eagerness to clear yourselves,*
> *what indignation, what alarm, what longing,*
> *what concern, what readiness . . .* [20]

I love those words: repentance, no regret, earnestness, eagerness, indignation, alarm, longing, concern, readiness. Those are words that any counselor would love to hear about a client who needed to change something significant. And they are words that any spouse would love to hear too. Much better words than guilty. They are motivating words, the kind that bring about change.

So here's another thing I want you to remember about being sorry: the kind of sorry that brings change is the "only for a little while"[21] kind. In Paul's discussion about the benefits of "godly sorrow," he makes the point that the hurt from their sorrow was short-lived. Healthy sorrow that brings about change lasts just long enough to change our hearts and teach us what we need to know. Then we need to be moving on.

The bottom line is this: when we feel sorry instead of guilty, we can focus on changing what's *wrong* instead of just trying to make the guilt feelings go away. Think about it: when we try to change because we feel guilty, we are just thinking about ourselves, trying to feel better about ourselves and not feel so bad.

But if, instead, we are *sorry* about the consequences of our behavior and how it affects God and the people we care about, then we are thinking about them. That is a motivation out of love and empathy instead of self-focused guilt; and love is the most powerful motivator of all. When people begin to focus on the ones they love and are affecting, they change.

So when you fall short, let yourself feel sorry that you have offended God or hurt another person or have done something destructive to yourself. Those are all people you care about, and that sorrow will help you make it right.

READY FOR A CHANGE?

So, hopefully you are tired of feeling guilty. If so, then the good news is that if you ask Jesus to forgive you and you believe in him—that he died for you and that God raised him from the dead to prove that he was who he said he was—then you can kiss guilt good-bye. You are totally forgiven, forever and ever. That is what the Bible calls being "in Christ." Here is what it says will happen if you believe in him:

> *In him we have redemption through his blood,*
> *the forgiveness of sins, in accordance*
> *with the riches of God's grace.*[22]

If you're ready for a change, you can begin right now. Today.

1. Ask for his forgiveness. The first step is to ask for his forgiveness. If you have never done that, just ask him right now.

"Jesus, I believe that you are the Son of God, that you died for me, and that you were raised from the dead for my sins. I have sinned in my life, and now I trust you for my forgiveness. Thank you for forgiving me."

You don't have to use those exact words; just speak from your own heart and tell him you want his forgiveness. That is what's important. If you do that, you have it.

2. Confess to God. Confess everything you can think of that you have done wrong. Write it down if that helps. Pour it all out. Tell him how you feel about it. Then tell him you are turning from all that and you want to be totally cleansed. Do as the scripture below says, then take the paper and burn it, celebrating his forgiveness. It is done. Over. You are clean.

> *If we confess our sins to God,*
> *he can always be trusted to forgive us and take our sins away.* [23]

3. Believe it! Read verses about your new relationship, daily if you have to, until you get it. Thank God for it. Talk to him about it. Write verses down about God's forgiveness, and memorize them. Get his Word into your head and heart. Then, whenever you have doubts, read the verses again. It may take a while, but the Bible says to hide his Word in your heart and meditate on it.

4. Talk to a friend or someone safe. Talk to someone you trust about the things you feel guilty about. Doing so will help you feel whole and healed:

> *Confess your sins to each other*
> *and pray for each other so that*
> *you can live together whole and healed.* [24]

Sometimes even after God has forgiven you, you need to feel that grace from one of his representatives, another person you can trust. This helps to internalize God's care for you. As you feel that person's acceptance, you will accept yourself as God does.

Secrets about Go

If you still have the accusing, critical voices in your head, you might want to talk to someone about where those come from. Often they are the voices from old relationships you have taken inside yourself, and now they sound like you. Really, they are old messages, and it is time to rework them and get them out. Get insight into whose voice you're really hearing—a parent, teacher, or someone who made you feel bad—and begin to disagree with them and get them out of your head. The more insight you have and the more you talk it out and disagree with those voices, the weaker they will become.

5. *Daily apply God's forgiveness.* Then daily as you walk through life and sin and make mistakes, apply God's forgiveness. Confess it to him immediately, and then claim his forgiveness. Remember the verse above . . . if you confess it, you are forgiven and your sins are *taken away.* Gone. Right then, right there. So, no extended guilties for hours or days. Let it go. Just like you received his forgiveness the first time, walk in it every day and enjoy your freedom from guilt.

6. *Live free!* And last, hold your head up high! Live free. Walk through life without shame or guilt, and realize that you have a brand-new start, each and every day. You are now not guilty!

You Can Trust God's Sovereignty

Aren't two sparrows sold for only a penny?
But your Father knows when any one of them falls to the ground.
Even the hairs on your head are counted.
So don't be afraid!
You are worth much more than many sparrows.

—MATTHEW 10:29–31 CEV

I remember when my spiritual mentors in college taught me about the sovereignty of God. I was depressed over a hand injury that resulted in my having to give up playing golf, which was a big loss for me. I was a brand-new Christian, and I was trying to figure out what to do next. This is what they told me: "God is in control. He knows about your hand, and he knows the desire of your heart and has allowed this injury to change your course. Whether or not he *willed* this to happen, we can't know, but you can bet that he has something good in store for you in the future." And I remember them saying something I was clueless about: "You have to learn to trust in the *sovereignty* of God."

They were telling me to "Trust in the fact that God is in control of the path of your life. It will be better than what you could have designed for yourself, even if you cannot see it now. God can bring good out of every situation."

I thought that sounded a little nuts at the time, but I should have known better. As I look back now, I can see that God definitely was in control and had something much better in store for me that has been very meaningful and fulfilling. I learned about a verse back then that has shaped my outlook ever since.

> We know that God causes everything
> to work together for the good
> of those who love God and are called
> according to his purpose for them.[25]

As the years have gone by, and as people of faith will tell you, we learn to trust more and more in the fact that God is in control. As you grow in trust, life gets steadier—more certain. And even when things don't work out, you can remain optimistic and see life as the exciting adventure that it is. Whatever you are going through at any moment does not define your future. God does. He is in control of your present and your tomorrow.

What does *sovereignty* mean? As I eventually learned, *sovereign* means "ultimate and supreme power." In the Bible it is sometimes translated "Most High." It means that in your life there is no evil force, no person, no chance, no randomness, no anything that is higher than God—for he is the *most* high. So no matter what happens that is out of your control, he is still in control. You may lose an individual battle, but God will win the ultimate war.

One of the biggest differences in the Bible's view of life and many philosophies is its assertion that life is not random. Things do not just happen in a meaningless, purposeless way. The Bible would agree with *The Secret* in that there *is* a controlling force in the universe. But rather than that force's being our own thoughts and feelings (as *The Secret* asserts), the Bible teaches that God is in control of the entire world and that nothing happens without his knowledge and permission. As his child, your life is in his hands, and that allows you to give up control and *rest*.

However, this does not mean that God causes or purposes bad things to happen, so it sometimes makes people wonder *If God is in control, why do bad things happen?* The quick answer has to do with the issue of free will. Our ability to choose can be used in very healthy ways, or it can be used to harm ourselves and others.

But for now, we'll stick with the concept of the *sovereignty* of God, and we'll talk more about the effects of choice as we go along.

ISSUES OF CONTROL

While God alone is all-powerful, we do have a certain amount of power in our lives—the ability to exert control over the things that affect us. One of the marks of mental health is the degree to which people realize that they have control over their own lives and exercise that power to choose. For example, if you are being mistreated in a relationship or don't like your job, you are not a helpless victim. You need to know that you have choices and can exert some control over your life and take the appropriate steps to take care of yourself. That is good and natural. You can choose to separate from or leave or confront the person. You can choose to get your résumé in order and look for another job. You are not helpless. Knowing this is an important aspect to mental health and well-being.

But what about the things that we do *not* have control over or the things we do not have power to change? What do we do when a person chooses not to respond to our efforts, or when our boss fires or hurts us or something else happens that was not what we were going for? This is when we must remember that even if something is outside *our* control, it is never outside the sovereignty of God.

BE AT REST

Two of our most basic needs in life are security and control. When we feel secure, we do not worry much about control. Picture the restfulness that a little baby has as it lies on its mother's chest. It totally lets go of any need to protest, scream, fight, resist, fear, or worry. It gives up all control.

As a psychologist, I can tell you that there are few things more fundamental to your mental health, to functioning in life, and to your psychological well-being than this issue of control. So what happens to our well-being when we feel out of control?

If you look around you, you can see what happens. Do you

know anyone who is stressed and anxious about things that are not working out? Do you know "control freaks" who get all whacked out when they don't get their way? How are their relationships going? How is their psychological well-being? Not so great. They may feel good when things are going well, but when they aren't, the high-gear stress sets in. When they lose control, the peace and well-being goes away, and they go into fight mode until they feel like they are back in control.

Anxiety and relationship struggles are not the only issues when people feel out of control. For many, depression also becomes a problem. As mentioned earlier, one of the most researched realities in all of psychology and psychiatry is a concept called learned helplessness. It reveals that the more powerless people feel, the more likely they are to get depressed and the slower they are to recover. Since they feel they can't do anything about life, the randomness of uncontrollable events makes it all seem hopeless; so they sink into despair, often at the onset of one bad event.

> IF YOU KNOW THAT GOD IS IN CONTROL, NO ONE EVENT CAN MEAN DOOMSDAY FOR YOUR FUTURE.

But if you know that God is in control, no one event can mean doomsday for your future. In fact, the longer we walk with God, the better we understand that when something we want does not occur, it is often because God has something better in mind for us. We learn to trust his no because his yes is going to be even better.

Resting in God's sovereignty is one of the biggest helps for anxiety, control issues, relationship fears, relationship dysfunctions, depression, addictions, and reaching goals. When things do not go well, trusting that God is still on the throne and that it will be okay allows us to go through difficulties on a very different plane and with hope and optimism, even when we don't have control over what is happening around us.

THE POWER OF TRUST

So, how do you practice this secret?

First, *understand that life is not out of control and random.* True, bad things happen as a result of living in a fallen world and as a result of the evil choices people make. But that does not have to lead to despair, because those events do not rule life or the universe. God does. Think about this a lot. Read the Bible and you will see how this theme runs through it. In the stories of the Old Testament, even the ones where things are going badly for Israel and they feel like all is lost, God is still in control. Even if they are scattered to the ends of the earth, he is still in control and brings them back and gives them a land. He does the same for us as well.

Second, *when bad things happen and you feel afraid, remind yourself that God is still in control.* As you go through life, bad things will happen and you will have times when you are depressed, so remember this truth. Remind yourself of the fact that even when things don't go right, God is still in control of your life:

- when you do not get the job

- when you lose the job

- when you lose a relationship

- when you have an illness

- when you go through financial difficulty

- when someone rejects you

- when you experience a trauma or loss

- when little things do not work out that overstress you (your flight gets canceled, and you have to spend another night in that city)

- when your schedule does not allow for you to do something you feel is important to a goal or a relationship

These and a thousand other things, large and small, can devastate us if we don't remember that God is in control and we can rest in him.

Talk to your friends who are in the journey with you about it. Ask them to remind you of God's sovereignty. Listen to people's testimonies of how God has walked with them through difficulties and how they came out the other side.

Feel the feelings related to any event. If a loss is sad, feel sad. But do not give way to hopelessness. Do not let your feelings define the universe. For God is still in control, and he has a purpose for you that is very good.

Secrets about Go

GOD REQUIRES SOMETHING OF YOU

Keep his decrees and commands,
which I am giving you today,
so that it may go well with you.
—DEUTERONOMY 4:40 NIV

One of the worst things about being a psychologist and a parent is that when your own child displays immature behavior, you tend to look into the future and see dire consequences. When my daughters were younger and did not want to eat their broccoli or pick up their toys, for example, I would see drug addiction, prison terms, flunking out of college, and nine marriages. So I have to be careful or I'll be a nut case.

On the other hand, my psychology training does help me be aware of some things I want my children to do right from a young age so that the rest of life goes well for them. I had an experience like that just the other day with my six-year-old, Olivia. She was upset about something and pouting a bit, refusing to talk about what was bugging her. When I asked her about it, she sort of blew me off and just pouted a bit more. I looked down the corridor of time and thought, *Not a good scenario for her future relationships. If*

I don't like this, a future friend or husband probably won't either. Time for a little coaching.

So I asked her about the rule. "Okay, Livi. What is the thing to do if something is bothering you?"

"Say what it is. Talk about it," she said without looking up at me.

"Right. So, look at me . . . (pause) . . . Livi, look up at me and tell me what is wrong."

At that point, as if her muscles were made of molasses, she slowly, slowly raised her head and eyes and finally looked up at me. With just a little more coaxing, she opened up and told me why she was mad at her sister. We had a good talk, and she figured out what to do with her little sister so things could be better.

For her, it was all about the problem itself, the conflict. For me, I couldn't care less about the game they were playing and that day's particular outcome. What I cared about was that she become the kind of person she needs to become for *life to go well for her.* I do not want to see her grow up to be a noncommunicator without the skills to make a relationship work. So I made her belly up and obey. If she had refused, I would have sent her to time-out until she was ready to do it right.

This is not something I enjoyed or wanted to do. After all, Tiger Woods was playing the US Open that day on TV. I would rather have watched him than give a seminar on communication on a Saturday. But Olivia needed it, and I want the best for her, so there we were.

210

NOT OUR OWN GODS

One of the differences between *The Secret* or other New Age spiritual teachings and the Bible is that in those teachings there is no one to answer to but ourselves. But according to the Bible, we are not our own gods. God is. And he has certain ways he wants us to live. He is our Father, and he has definite requirements for us, just like any good parent. And that is the "getting off the bus" point for a lot of people; this is the reason many reject the God of the Bible.

We humans have a disease: We do not want to answer to anyone but ourselves about how we live. We want to have our own moral code that feels good for us and that we believe is right and has integrity. But the truth is, there is One greater than us to whom we have to answer. He just is. (To my way of thinking, believing the Bible on this point is not very hard. If you remember when you were born, the world was already here, so you probably were not the one who made it. At least that is how I think about it. I know I didn't do it. Someone else made it.)

THE BOTTOM LINE

But even when we don't want to do it—just as Olivia did not want to obey me and talk to me about what was bothering her—obeying God is good for us. We may not always like it, but it saves our lives. It's not hard to understand that children don't want to be under their parents' control. When we are "children" in our

211

faith walk, we, too, may fight against restrictions God places on our lives. But as we grow up a bit, we begin to see that they are for our own good. Being free from God's restrictions would ultimately do us in, because they are there for our own good.

Byrne makes a statement in *The Secret* that well captures what our attitude should be about God's laws. She says, "If you don't understand the law, it doesn't mean you should reject it."[26] She has a good grasp on a concept that many of us would do well to apply to God's laws. Just because we don't understand all of God's laws does not mean we should reject them. Someone may resent a stop sign and think, *I don't want a silly sign telling me what to do*. But what he thinks about that sign doesn't matter if it is warning about a cliff that is directly in front of him. If he doesn't obey, he's toast.

So God does have some requirements for us. Basically, "Don't drive off the cliff." In other words, he wants us to obey him so that it will go well for us. The psalmist David said,

> *Your laws are wonderful.*
> *No wonder I obey them!*[27]

According to the Bible, God is not just an energy or a force, but a person to be obeyed. When we obey him, things really do work out better, just like when we pay attention to gravity . . . or a nagging psychologist parent.

Secrets about God

ℰPILOGUE

I stand at the door and knock.
If you hear my voice and open the door,
I will come in, and we will share a meal together as friends.

REVELATION 3:20 NLT

My friend said something I think she meant as a passing comment, but it took us to a much deeper conversation.

"You know what I like about your faith?"

"No, what?" I said, not knowing she liked anything in particular.

"It seems to do so much for you and makes a lot of things work, and it makes sense. That is really cool. But what I like *most* is that you don't force it on people."

"Oh, I would never want to force it on people," I said. "I will share it with them, but certainly not force it. I think everyone has the right to believe whatever they believe."

"Right," she said. "That's what I mean. Like, it is true for you, but someone else's religion can be true too."

"Certainly there is some truth in lots of religions," I said. "But I do think that the one I believe is *true*."

"Right . . . true for you, but not necessarily true for everyone."

"What do you mean?" I asked.

"Well, it's not like yours is *right*, like *true-true*, and others are wrong."

"Actually, I do believe mine is true-true," I said. "Like it is *really* true. Like the real *truth*."

"Wait a minute," she said, "there's no such thing as *truth*."

"Including that statement?" I asked.

She just looked at me. "I never thought about it like that."

"Exactly," I said. "That statement falls in on itself. You cannot make that statement. There is truth and non-truth. You may think there is no such thing as truth, but if you jump off the roof, you will find that gravity is not just true for me. It is true-true for you too.

"But let me tell you why I know the Bible's faith is true-true. I have a problem, and you do too. Here it is: There was a man who said he was God. He said we could know he was God by testing his ways to see if they are true. He also said he would do miracles and prove he was God by his power. And then he said the ultimate proof would be that people would kill him and he would come back from the dead.

"Then he did all of that in real space-time history. Some people now try to dispute what he did and explain it away, but there were just too many eyewitnesses who lived on to tell about it—and some who died for it—to think that it did not happen. There are also people who testify to his being alive today. So my problem, and yours, is answering the question: *what am I going to do with this man?* What are you going to do with someone who says he is God and proves it?

"My answer has been to follow him. I am a psychologist, and I have put a lot of people into hospitals who've had grandiose fantasies. But this one, Jesus of Nazareth, I believe. I believe he is the Force behind it all, the God of the universe, and that his ways are true and that they make life work. And I believe he is alive and still has the power to do miracles in our lives today. That is why I believe he is true-true."

And that is what I hope you find, as well as the *answers* to the three questions we raised in the Welcome of this book:

1. The Force behind the universe is not impersonal, but personal.

2. There is a set of laws he has given us that make life work; and when we try them, we will know they are true, and they will set us free.

3. Life is not all up to you, after all. It is to be lived in relationship with your Creator. He is looking for you. If you seek him, you will find him and all the other secrets of God.

God bless you,
Henry Cloud, PhD
Los Angeles, CA
2007

NOTES

WELCOME
1. See Acts 17:24–29
2. 1 Corinthians 4:1 NIV

THE SEARCH
1. Matthew 6:33 NIV
2. Matthew 6:34 NIV

THE SECRET REVEALED
1. Psalm 143:7 *The Message*
2. Psalm 9:10 NIV
3. Hebrews 11:6 NLT
4. Matthew 7:7

THE KEY TO ALL OTHER SECRETS
1. See Hebrews 11:6
2. Rhonda Byrne, *The Secret* (New York: Atria Books, 2006), 81.
3. Hebrews 11:8 NLT
4. Matthew 27:46 NIV
5. Job 13:15 KJV
6. 1 Thessalonians 4:13 NLT
7. See Matthew 4:7
8. See John 14:9
9. See James 2:17
10. See Deuteronomy 5:29

SECRETS ABOUT HAPPINESS
1. Ecclesiastes 4:9–12 NIV
2. Colossians 2:2 NASB
3. Philippians 2:2 NIV

4. 1 Samuel 18:1 NIV
5. Here are just a few scriptures from the NIV that show what the Bible says about our thoughts and our hearts: Philippians 2:5—"Your attitude should be the same as that of Christ Jesus"; 3:13–14—"Forgetting what is behind and straining toward what is ahead, I press on toward the goal"; 4:6—"Do not be anxious about anything, but in everything, by prayer . . ."; 4:8—"whatever is true, . . . noble, . . . right, . . . pure, . . . lovely, . . . admirable . . . think about such things"; Colossians 3:1—"set your hearts on things above"; 3:2—"set your minds on things above"; 3:15—"Let the peace of Christ rule in your hearts"; 3:16—"Let the word of Christ dwell in you richly."
6. 2 Corinthians 10:5
7. 2 Corinthians 10:5 *The Message*
8. Martin Seligman, *Learned Optimism* (New York: Free Press, 1998).
9. See 2 Corinthians 10:5 *The Message*
10. 2 Corinthians 10:5 NASB
11. Romans 8:38–39 NLT
12. Romans 8:28 NLT
13. Hebrews 13:5–6 NIV
14. Proverbs 23:18 NIV
15. Psalm 112:7 NIV

The Secret Things of Go

16. Aaron Beck, *Cognitive Therapy of Depression* (New York: Guilford Press, 1987).

17. Psalm 37:4 NIV

18. Proverbs 13:19 NIV

19. Proverbs 26:13 *The Message*

20. See John 13:34; Romans 12:10; 15:7; Ephesians 4:2; 4:32; Colossians 3:13; 1 Thessalonians 5:11; 1 Peter 1:22; 1 John 4:7

21. See Numbers 13:30

22. Deuteronomy 6:21 NIV

23. 2 Corinthians 3:17 NIV

24. See Romans 8:6, 9

25. Galatians 5:23

26. Deuteronomy 6:3 NIV

27. Philippians 4:13 NIV

28. 1 Corinthians 10:13 NLT

29. See Galatians 6:1

30. Matthew 5:4 NASB

31. Mark 7:20–23 *The Message*

32. 1 John 1:7–9 NLT

33. Colossians 3:13 CEV

34. Matthew 7:24–27 NIV

35. James 1:2–5 *The Message*

SECRETS ABOUT RELATIONSHIPS

1. Luke 6:31 NASB

2. Romans 12:21 NIV

3. Proverbs 18:21 NIV

4. See 1 Peter 4:10

5. Jeremiah 22:3 *The Message*

6. Matthew 25:40 NIV

7. See Matthew 7:17, 20

8. Matthew 7:17, 20 NLT

9. Psalm 101:3–7 NLT

10. Hebrews 5:14 NASB

11. Matthew 7:6 NASB

12. Matthew 5:23–24 *The Message*

13. Matthew 18:15 *The Message*

14. Proverbs 12:26 NIV

SECRETS ABOUT FULFILLING YOUR PURPOSE

1. Psalm 100:3 NIV

2. Ecclesiastes 3:12–13 NIV

3. Ecclesiastes 2:24–25 NIV

4. Matthew 16:25 NIV

5. Proverbs 16:9 NIV

6. See Mark 12:30–31

7. Byrne, 8.

8. Matthew 7:16–20 NIV

9. Matthew 12:33 NIV

10. Ecclesiastes 11:1 NIV

11. See Proverbs 10:4; 13:3, 4, 21; 14:15, 23; 22:3

12. See Hebrews 12:7

13. James 1:2 NASB

14. NKJV; emphasis added

15. Proverbs 13:3 *The Message*

16. Proverbs 13:4 CEV

17. Proverbs 13:21 CEV

18. See 2 Chronicles 2

19. See 1 Corinthians 12; Romans 12:4–7

20. Proverbs 15:22 *The Message*

21. Psalm 25:5, 12–13 NLT

22. Matthew 25:24–28 NLT

23. See Genesis 1:27

24. Matthew 7:7 NIV

25. 2 Chronicles 31:21

26. Luke 18:2–5 NIV

SECRETS ABOUT GOD

1. John M. Gottman, Ph.D., and Nan Silver, *The Seven Principles for Making Marriage Work* (New York: Three Rivers Press, 2000; originally published by Crown, 1999).

2. 1 Peter 5:7 NIV

3. Psalm 55:22 NIV
4. See Romans 8:15
5. John 15:9 NIV
6. John 15:7 NIV
7. See James 1:13–17
8. Ephesians 2:10 NIV
9. Psalm 37:4 NLT
10. See James 4:3
11. James 4:2 NIV
12. Romans 8:31 NIV
13. John 12:47 NIV
14. Acts 10:43 NIV
15. Romans 8:1 NASB
16. Verse 7 NIV
17. John 8:10–11 NIV
18. See Romans 8:1
19. Psalm 32:3 NIV
20. 2 Corinthians 7:10–11 NIV
21. 2 Corinthians 7:8 NIV
22. Ephesians 1:7 NIV
23. 1 John 1:9 CEV
24. James 5:16 *The Message*
25. Romans 8:28 NLT
26. Byrne, 21.
27. Psalm 119:129 NLT

The Secret Things of Go